ISBN 978-1-105-90950-4

Red Panda Publishing, Inc. via SOAR Association. Collaboratively orchestrated in union with *Student Observation and Research* academic journal editorial board.

BINGHAMTON – BROOME – CORNELL – CORTLAND
ITHACA – TOMPKINS

FROM WITHIN THE BORDERLAND
THE IMMATERIALISM OF GENDER AND THE ILLUSION OF CONTROLLED NARRATIVES

CONTENTS

10 1. Essentialism and the Surface Level Understanding of the Human Race

17 2. Justice, Care, and Morality: The Immediate Failure of Essentialist Understandings

23 3. Gender and Power Within Shakespeare's *Much Ado About Nothing*

31 4. Damned if He Does, Damned if He Doesn't: A Look at Chaucer's Portrayal of Women in *The Canterbury Tales*

49 5. The Highs and Lows in the Treatment of Female Figures

54 6. A Full Circle Examination of Female Oppression in Bharati Mukherjee's *Jasmine*

64 7. Similar Beginnings, Yet Differing Ends in *Sister Carrie* and *Maggie: A Girl of the Streets*

71 8. Postmodern Memory in Toni Morrison's *Beloved* and Christopher Nolan's *Memento*

83 9. A Historical Look at Jane Austen's *Sense and Sensibility*

93 10. Modern Masculinity and the Use of Groups and Structured Dominance for Power

102 11. A Child of His Times: Immanuel Kant and Enlightenment

108 12. Power as Defined by Relationships With Men

115 13. Sir Gawain's Numerous Portrayals in Regards to Masculinity

123 14. A Glimpse Into the Scholarship Surrounding Entertainment and Realism Within Medieval Drama

130 15. John Donne's Bold New Cosmological Model in "The Sun Rising"

140 16. Looking Deeper Into Issues Within Wordsworth's "The world is too much with us"

144 17. Slavery and Revolution in Blake's *America: a Prophecy*

161 18. Contrasting Behaviors of Minor Characters in Stephen Crane's *The Monster*

166 19. Comparing Sins in J. M. Synge's *The Tinker's Wedding*

174 20. Relating Postsecular Properties in *The English Patient* and *The Matrix*

187 21. The History and Ever-Changing Identity of Masculinity Studies

198 "The Men of the Valley and Their Defining Masochism"

"This book, then, speaks to my existence. My preoccupations with the inner life of the Self, and with the struggle of that Self amidst adversity and violation; with the confluence of primordial images; with the unique positionings consciousness takes at these confluent streams; and with my almost instinctive urge to communicate, to speak, to write about life on the borders, life in the shadows." - From the third edition of Gloria Anzaldua's Borderlands: La Frontera. *California: Aunt Lute Books, 1987. Print.*

1. Essentialism and the Surface Level Understanding of the Human Race

Man Without Constraints

With much of the human race in constant pursuit of improvement, many concepts have been introduced and removed from society throughout time. Thanks to this process, some concepts have been left behind and enshrined within textbooks as relics of history. However, among the outdated philosophical ideas left stagnant by the educated minds of the present, one concept was oddly resurrected in the contemporary era of scholarship. The idea, named "essentialism" by Aristotle, is that all human beings share defining traits. Its resurrection and inspection by scholars has reconfirmed the belief that this idea is outdated and belongs in the past, especially with the rise of civil rights. No matter what the support or justification, the concept does not function in a thinking world, because it is woefully ignorant of its misuse throughout history. Proclaiming, as Aristotle did, that we are all linked by a common thread is misleading, and works only to exclude others and include a select, chosen few of the planet's intricate beings. Being unable to be defined or compartmentalized is what makes us human, not the ability to be generalized or compacted into a surface level understanding.

The progression of understanding and the acceptance of difference, stemming from various civil rights moments, has begun to teach those within the dominant how to accept others. Within some circles, cultures whose traditions differ from that of the dominant's are accepted as equal. While this may appear to be wholly good, it is not without its conflicts. In looking back and reexamining ancient texts, contemporary scholars took to what they considered a particularly troubling text: Aristotle's *Nicomachean Ethics*. Within this text is the primary focus of what Aristotle calls "essentialism." In brief, essentialism is the idea that all human beings must share base level traits that, in a way, unite them. Critics have responded that there can be no defining traits, because it is self-defeating to have only a handful of signs that one is or is not human. However, despite the wave of criticism, not every scholar is against the idea of essentialism.

It can be argued that these universal traits that contemporary scholars denounce are able to be defended and explained. In her text titled "Human Functioning and Social Justice: In Defense of Aristotelian Essentialism," Martha Nussbaum argues for the idea of essentialism. She explains that she understands it as, "the view that human life has certain central defining features" (Nussbaum 205). However, it is the use of words such as "certain" and "central" that have critics skeptical. The idea that there can only be a certain amount of defining features for human beings as a whole is insulting not only to microscopic minorities located around the globe, but also the idea of what it means to be human. Part of the beauty of the human race is its intricacy and its inability to be summarized. It is outside the bounds of language, no matter how many the central defining features. In addition, there is no accurate way of determining what is central to the human race as a whole. The majority cannot accurately speak for a minority group, and minority groups cannot speak for each other without the risk of compartmentalizing. Essentialism is a lazy approach to the complex topic of the human race.

Those who side with essentialist understandings of the human race are damaging in promoting their surface level understanding of others. Nussbaum claims that, despite what opponents to the approach say, there is no, "ignorance of history" (205). However, it is difficult to argue otherwise.

While it may first seem extreme to say that the approach is, "in league with racism and sexism," it most certainly is within these categories (205). When there are some traits that are considered more important to others, the dividing lines are drawn. Additionally, arguing that "relativism is taken to be a recipe for social progress" with a sarcastic tone dulls down the credibility of Nussbaum's reasoning (205). When the traits that define humans are regarded as being relative, it is then that the road to understanding can be traveled. No person has to fit a certain mold in order to be labeled a human being. Furthermore, with western society's heightened understanding and appreciation for otherness, it is no wonder that "contemporary assaults on "essentialism" and on nonrelative accounts of human functioning have recently made a dramatic appearance" (203). This rise in attacks against generalizations can again be attributed to the progression of civil rights within Western society. Nussbaum labels this rise in political correctness "antiessentialism," but it can instead be labeled what it truthfully is: the understanding that the human race in its entirety cannot be generalized in the slightest (204). It is not a matter of being politically correct, but, rather, correct. Further in the text, Nussbaum attempts to breakdown the whole of essentialism into two branches: internalist essentialism and metaphysical essentialism.

The idea of essentialism is comprised of several subtopics, each of which can be examined separately. The primary two types of essentialism are internalist and metaphysical. Rather than elaborating on the vast and complex topic of metaphysical essentialism, or the idea that "the world is apart from the interpretive workings of the cognitive faculties of living beings," she instead shifts to its more simplistic companion topic (206). By stripping away trivial properties and focusing on the basic traits that unite us, internalist essentialism allows for a human relationship based around commonalities. She explains how, "the deepest examination of human history and human cognition *from within* still reveals a more or less determinate account of the human being" (207). Additionally, instead of bending to the

12

arguments of her critics, she reinforces her belief in the concept. She believes that, without essentialism, the human race is, "deprived of two moral sentiments that are absolutely necessary if we are to live together decently in the world: compassion and respect" (205). However, there is nothing less compassionate or respectful than breaking intricate cultures away from their uniqueness and compartmentalizing them into a universal, bland space.

In an attempt to deflect the criticisms from her antiessentialist opponents, Nussbaum lays out her argument piece by piece in order to explain her position. The first question she addresses is, "How does one pick out some elements of human life and label them as more fundamental than others?" (208). Immediately, she brings awareness to her opponents' trump card. No matter what the answer, nor how carefully worded the response, the aforementioned question cannot be addressed without being self-defeating. To put it simply, what qualifies a person as human and what does not? In addition, once these qualities are established, how can they be legitimate? Aside from the intricacies of the world's cultures is the way the world's cultures forge their understandings. These, "people, it is claimed, understand human life and humanness in widely different ways, and any attempt to produce a list of "essential properties" is bound to enshrine certain understandings of the human and to demote others" (208). Without a doubt, it is at this point in the process that the most dominant group would take over, and the minority groups are quieted or even silenced. The only way a neglect of historical and cultural differences could be averted is to achieve an unanimous agreement, and such a task would be nearly impossible given the difference between the people of the world.

Among the opponents of essentialism is a fear that the dominant group's opinion would overrule that of others, and that the scene would promote historical ignorance. It is explained that the process would neglect, "the radical otherness of [minorities] by bringing [dominant] Western essentialist values into the picture" (203). In this moment, there must be an ignorance of history, because the colonizer is typically unable to think on the same wavelength as the colonized. Of course, the human race shares certain traits at certain times, such as an appreciation for our young, but then there is the issue about the recorded instances of infanticide in Sparta and elsewhere. The same outcome applies to love, as well. There is the issue of having many wives in present day Africa, or gang members having no committed relationships in areas such as Compton, California or Camden, New Jersey. Lastly, even an appreciation for life is not universal. Mafia members, gang members, sociopaths, drug dealers and many more groups are often feared for their disregard of human life. To break down the pointlessness of universal traits, even goodness is an issue. Simply asking multiple groups to define "good" conjures up varying ideas of what it means to do good, because it is an ideal. These outcomes reveal that there is not only a historical ignorance present in the process, but also a plain ignorance.

At this point, it is important to remember that this concept was developed by a man who, according to Nussbaum, thought that "women and slaves were not full-fledged human beings" (209). They were excluded from being human, because they did not fit the mold, just as many groups have also been regarded as less than human by the various dominant powers throughout time. Additionally, Nussbaum herself admits that "The Aristotelian conception can indeed be *prejudicially applied*. It is possible to say all the right things about humanness and then to deny that women or blacks or other minorities fall under the concept" (226). These practices are the sort of dehumanization that African and Jewish groups, for example, have been subjected to for over two thousand years. To all oppressed people over the span of time, a statement such as this is the ultimate instance of stating the obvious. The idea of essentialism is an outdated reminder of the bigotry and absentmindedness that used to rule over the land, even if unintentionally.

In the various books of *Nicomachean Ethics*, Aristotle himself provides fuel for critics and others in opposition of the idea. Early in the text, Aristotle ponders if happiness comes by virtue or chance. Upon considering the two possibilities, he arrives at the conclusion that it must be god-given,

14

because, "it is the best" (Book 1, Part 9). Immediately, he puts one value over another, illustrating the futility of ranking the human race's defining traits. However, he takes it a step further by stating that the trait, "seems to be common to all species and not specifically human" (Book 1, Part 13). This surface level understanding of commonalities may not pose such a threat to animals, but for minorities throughout history, it certainly has. To further explain what he means, Aristotle then entirely lays out what it means to be good, and how to become good. These processes, as critics have noted, typically only refer to men. Aristotle notes how, "without doing these no one would have a prospect of becoming good" (Book 2, Part 4). Again, there is some sort of criteria to meet, or task to achieve in order to become something as universally applied as goodness. Furthermore, he demonstrates his preference towards men. For example, upon committing adultery, Aristotle explains, "He acts unjustly, then, but is not unjust" (Book 5, Part 6). He expands this by noting how, "a man is not a thief, yet he stole, not an adulterer, yet he committed adultery; and similarly in all other cases" (Book 5, Part 6). Thanks to these instances and the excuses provided in order to explain them, the idea that the human race can be defined has defeated itself. When listing off what it means to be good, even, Aristotle himself displays a bias that tips the scales in favor of one group over another. Coincidentally, the favored group just so happens to be the sex in power at the time *Nicomachean Ethics* was written.

The beauty and appreciation for the human race stems not from a supposed common thread that unites us all, but rather the reality that no such thread can exist. Essentialism is a self-defeating idea that plays no part in a world of compassionate and respectful humans, or thinking, rational humans for that matter. No matter what the example provided, there is no one single belief or idea that unites the entirety of the human race. Rather, there can only ever be a common thread that unites fractions of the population and creates borders from the rest of the human race. This practice was exercised throughout history, with a dominant group typically attempting to establish

15

what made a person right or wrong, or fit their mold. However, the reality is that there are no qualifiers for being human, because, once there are, they are immediately abused. The very fluctuation in what it means to be human over the years is further proof that it is only a simple definition that can be altered and transformed to fit the needs of the dominant. With that being said, it can be asserted that essentialism is a relic of the past, and remains a stagnant topic. For those who disagree with the concept, they are simply stating the obvious, and those who agree with the concept promote a hurtful, historically ignorant and self-defeating surface level understanding of the human race.

SOURCES

Aristotle. *Nicomachean Ethics*. Written 350 B.C.E. Translated by W. D. Ross. Massachusetts Institute of Technology, 2009. Accessed 15 Feb. 2012. Web.

Nussbaum, Martha. "Human Functioning and Social Justice: In Defense of Aristotelian Essentialism." *Political Theory* 20.2 (1992): 202-246. Web.

2. Justice, Care, and Morality: The Immediate Failure of Essentialist Understandings

Man Beyond Universalism

It is often the case, thanks to the intricacies and complexities of the modern and globally-aware world, that people tend to desire a concrete result from within a gray area full of ambiguities. What is desired is clarity, or a universal understanding to an issue that is not always so simple. One such issue is morality and the dilemmas by which it is surrounded. Some researchers and writers tend to examine justice and care, two intimate issues within morality, and attempt to speak about them with universal and absolute tones. Presenting two opposing sides of this same issue are Carol Gilligan and Joan Tronto, who argue that morals can never be universal given complexities, and that attitudes towards morality are strict and engendered, respectively. The result is that, while there is always an attempt being made to achieve an essentialist-styled, universal trait for a certain group of people, it is a futile practice, because it cannot be done accurately or successfully.

More often than not, people prefer to view something ambiguous in one way more than another. Whether it means there are two ways of viewing, or more, one way dominates immediately and remains what is seen more readily from there on out. In her text titled "Moral Orientation and Moral Development," Carol Gilligan immediately describes this phenomenon. She explains, "When one looks at an ambiguous figure like the drawing that can be seen as a young or old woman, or the image of the vase and the faces, one initially sees it in only one way. Yet even after seeing it in both ways, one way often seems more compelling" (Gilligan 31). This process of perception does not exist only within the realm of sight. In fact, the same process is found to occur with morals as well. Gilligan calls this phenomenon, "perceptual organization" (31). In other words, people will tend to see or judge things in

17

one way over another, no matter how many alternatives of which they are made aware. It is because of this that any attempt at achieving an essentialist, absolute understanding of anything is futile. It cannot be done, and this is especially the case with morals.

The key issue with morals and the attempt to label them with absolutes is that they are altered with the slightest of conditional change. Gilligan states that, like the way we view and judge everything in our environments, "a similar phenomenon with respect to moral judgment" occurs (31). Before venturing into the way people tend to make moral judgments and the conditions that affect them, it is important to understand why there is a desire to categorize. Gilligan states that "moral judgments organize thinking about choice in difficult situations" (32). Given that these situations could be life-altering, or even life-threatening, what often clouds the situation is a moral gray area. In other words, ambiguity makes for many decisions to be made with moral justification. However, what tends to override evaluating the complex situation and considering the sometimes numerous competing alternatives is, "the wish for clarity" (32). This wish for clarity, whether it is driven by power and control or just laziness, tends to result in a absolute understanding of something. It is due to this that people tend to take on, "the position that there is one right or better way to think about moral problems" (32). Yet, only after it is understood that there is no one way of judging anything, especially thanks to how easily perspectives can change opinions, that compartmentalization is revealed as being useless. Furthermore, Gilligan explains that everyone is subject to change. She feels that "everyone is vulnerable both to oppression and abandonment" in some form or another (32). Any sort of oppression or abandonment can result in, "a shift in perspective," or "a change in moral orientation" (34). This process can be told through classic stories such as the rich man who visits the slums and experiences judgment from the people, or the poor girl who gets swept off her feet by the wealthy prince, only to realize the difference between the classes and their sufferings. While not every shift in perspective needs to be so monumental, even slight shifts can radically alter the way a person judges a situation.

When it comes to judging even justice and care themselves, what results after examination are not clear cut lines and obvious barriers, but rather more of a gray area. Gilligan states how, "justice and care as moral perspectives are not opposites or mirror-images of one another, with justice uncaring and care unjust" (34). In other words, justice and care are never one simple thing. Rather, they are like anything else in that they can have many different meanings, or even occupy the same meaning. In addition, both care and justice can affect the other. To some, "within a justice construction, care becomes the mercy that tempers justice" (36). For others, justice plagues mercy and rules it out as a force that diminishes justice. The two sides of morality are not separate, but are instead two sides of the same coin. They reflect, influence and intertwine with each other, unable to be the clear-cut and isolated.

In favor of absolute and one-size-fits-all understandings, it is often assumed a certain gender or type of person judge a moral dilemma in a certain manner. Yet, this assumption is disproved once more by Gilligan, and it is thanks to a powerful factor: pressure from family and friends (35). No matter what the stereotype for the type of person, one overriding factor becomes peer pressure. While it is thought that feminine types prefer care and masculine types prefer justice, the inclusion of friends and family in the matter throws off the entire situation. Gilligan explains how, "the moral question becomes how to maintain moral principles or standards and resist the influence of one's parents or friends" (35). For example, on the topic of execution, a woman may be conflicted if she prefers correction and teaching over capital punishment, while her family and friends do not. She is put in the tough position of staying true to her own morals, while remaining acceptable in the eyes of her friends and family. One such example of this conflict is what Gilligan names the "abortion dilemma." Gilligan notes how, "the abortion dilemma arises because there is no way not to act, and no way of acting that does not alter the connection between self and others" (36). No matter what the issue, the inclusion and influence of others on one's own decision results in no one way to act.

The effects of training and lifestyles is one last nail in the coffin of assuming certain types of people have only one way to act. While gender differences were, "parallel to those previously reported, with boys more often spontaneously using and preferring justice solutions and girls more often spontaneously using and preferring care solutions," it is important to consider the effects of class and lifestyle (39). Class and finance, sexual orientation, and even religious affiliation can have an influence on moral dilemmas and opinions. For example, according to Gilligan, poorer and weaker types, "learn what it means to depend on the authority and the good will of others" (40). On the contrary, the wealthy and powerful do not associate themselves with such matters, but instead focus on power, control and justice (40). The same things can be said for homosexuals in hostile neighborhoods, or members of an undesirable religion located within a hateful community. What sort of wealth a person is born into, their sexual orientation and nearly every other factor of a person's life is considered and judged in relation to others. The end result is a near infinite number of complexities and intricacies that clearly show that there is never one way any person should act or think.

Competing with the ideas of Gilligan is the thought that caring and power are absolute and universal properties. They are borderline essentialist properties, suggesting that certain types of people act in certain ways. Joan Tronto states in her text "Women and Caring: What Can Feminists Learn About Morality and Caring?" that certain traits are certainly engendered. She explains how, "Men care about money, career, ideas, and advancement; men show they care by the work they do, and the values they hold, and the provisions they make for their families" (Tronto 101). These properties appear to be taught, and not universal. Rather, they are the suggested ways a man is supposed to act, as opposed to being how every man instinctively acts. Reinforcing this is her further statement, "Women care for their families,

20

neighbors, and friends; women care for their families by doing the direct work of caring" (101). While this sort of act is often called the "labor of love," it is still centered around emotions; the sort of thing stereotypically applied to women. What Tronto appears to do is not push the boundaries of understanding morals and caring, but instead refers back to centuries-old engendered attributes.

It is important, when examining the supposed differences between men and women in relation to justice and care, to define what it means to care for and about something. Tronto explains how, "Caring about refers to less concrete objects" (103). According to her, it is a love for immaterial things. Men are associated with this, because what is cared about is success, and other things which cannot be physically grasped. On the other hand is caring for something, which Tronto states is more associated with women. She writes, "caring for involves responding to the particular, concrete, physical, spiritual, intellectual, psychic, and emotional needs of others" (103). There is a fascination with, "the self, another person, or a group" (103). This idea would explain why women always appear to care for a person, or a group of people, such as their families. As a result of these definitions and how Tronto has applied them to certain sexes, she states that "caring is engendered" (103). However, this idea was thoroughly defeated by Gilligan and others, thanks to the many examples used to illuminate the fact that no one person acts in any one way. What Tronto presents are not facts, but rather assumptions based on stereotypes.

The willingness to apply universal traits to a certain group of people is understandable, with the vast intricacies that a globally-minded world presents, but it is not possible without being highly inaccurate. Gilligan has explained how people's positions within society affect their views on issues and their moral judgment. Whether their views and understandings are based on race, religion, financial status or even sexual orientation, just about every little aspect of a person's life affects how they think. The result is that, for example, men and women never think in any one way about anything. To state otherwise is immediately inaccurate, and the opinion cannot be sustained without seeming out of touch with the world's cultural and societal complexities.

SOURCES

Gilligan, Carol. "Moral Orientation and Moral Development." *Justice and Care*. Ed. Virginia Held. Colorado: Westview Press, 1995. 31-46. Print.

Tronto, Joan. "Women and Caring: What Can Feminists Learn About Morality and Caring?" *Justice and Care*. Ed. Virginia Held. Colorado: Westview Press, 1995. 101-115. Print.

3. Gender and Power Within Shakespeare's *Much Ado About Nothing*

Man as the Orchestrator

The debate on what it means to be powerful presents numerous complexities. In Shakespeare's *Much Ado About Nothing*, many characters possess powerful traits, yet critics disagree on the subject. For example, Carol Cook's essay, "The Sign and Semblance of Her Honor," attempts to prove that it is Hero who is most powerful. However, numerous other critics say otherwise, and state that figures such as Leonato and Claudio are powerful. Given the evidence provided by the play itself, Hero is an indisputably weak character. She is made into an object to possess by the men of the play, and is unable to have any influence over her own marriage. The only woman with power is her cousin, Beatrice, who is able to command Benedick, and perform other masculine actions. Furthermore, the power of the men in the play does not fully match Carol Cook's theory. Both Claudio and Leonato are especially powerful, and have the ability to control others and make demands. In Shakespeare's *Much Ado About Nothing*, power rests in the hands of most of the male characters, leaving Beatrice as the only female to slightly taste power.

Carol Cook provides for a unique view of Shakespeare's *Much Ado About Nothing* in her essay, "The Sign and Semblance of Her Honor." She states that Shakespeare's play is less about female inferiority as it is littered with, "...pervasive masculine anxiety..." (Cook 186). The focus of her article is that the male dominance within the play is actually a form of weakness. She believes the men of the play to be filled with an anxiety which keeps them paranoid and fearful of being cheated on. Carol Cook notes that said male dominance is made present by the, "...sword, and the phallus..." (Cook 186). Aside from the actions of the males in the play, Cook notes that there are quite a few phallic symbols. Additionally, many elements in the play are centered around, "...masculine privilege and masculine aggression..." (Cook 186). All of this aggression, dominance, and masculinity add up to fear and anxiety in Carol Cook's eyes. According to Cook, all men have an, "...anxiety about women's potential power over men..." (Cook 187). Furthermore, it is Hero who, "...is the focus of masculine anxieties" (Cook 190). Although Hero is the most silent character in the play, she is the most endangering to the men of the play. Moreover, though many critics and readers of *Much Ado About Nothing* say otherwise, Carol Cook believes Hero is the most powerful character within the play, and Claudio is one of the weakest. I strongly disagreed with these claims, and feel as if Carol Cook's concept of power is off by a large degree. The men of the play are truly powerful and dominating forces, while the women are mere objects to be acted upon.

It is very important that the very concept of power is defined before the explanation of who is most and least powerful in *Much Ado About Nothing* is initiated. By definition and my own personal understanding, power is defined by control. The methods of control can come in various fashions both big and small. First, powerful people have great amounts of influence over others. For example, Beatrice is powerful as she tells Benedick to kill Claudio, and he simply agrees. Don John is another example of someone who influences people. Second, power is defined by authority. Though Don Pedro is royalty, Leonato stands alone in terms of authority as he is the undeniable ruler of the estate. All characters within the play must take orders from Leonato, and this renders him as being powerful. Another element of power is political strength. For example, Don Pedro is royalty, therefore he has the ability to influence, control and command vast amounts of people. Lastly, the ability to do or act defines how powerful a person is. All of the men within the play act, and most of the women within the play are acted upon. Carol Cook's article supports this as she states that "It is the place of the woman to be the object..." (Cook 189). In conclusion, being acted upon defines the women of the play as being weak, and not powerful in comparison to the men.

In terms of female power, Beatrice is by far the most powerful as she has numerous masculine traits. Carol Cook states Beatrice wields phallic wit, or the wit of men (Cook 190). When arguing with Benedick, she is able to quickly craft witty responses. For example, she makes fun of Benedick by stating, "Scratching could not make it worse and 'twere such a face as yours were" (Shakespeare 7). She is even able to overwhelm Benedick, and surpass his intelligent insults. William Babula makes note of her power as she able to label Benedick, "...a dummy" (Babula 10). This ability to respond to Benedick's insults demonstrates how she can perform actions and act freely. Unlike the other women of the play, Beatrice is mostly free of social constraints. For example, she resists the idea of marriage until the end of the play, and this sets her apart from the other women. She does not allow herself to be controlled by any male character for quite a great deal of time. Another event in which she displays her power is through her ability to command and influence Benedick. This is astonishing considering that, with all sexism and patriarchal beliefs aside, men were undoubtedly more powerful than women in this time period. This fact renders her ability to command a man incredible. However, her one very minor weakness is that she is unable to kill Claudio herself, but instead has to have a man do it for her. In conclusion, Beatrice's unique traits leave her standing alone as the only woman in the play with the powers of a man. She is not simply a powerful woman, but the only woman in the play with any power whatsoever.

Of the women in *Much Ado About Nothing*, Hero is the second weakest. Throughout the play, she is nothing more than an object to be commanded by the men. As a result, she is without any traits associated with power. Moreover, she barely speaks a word in even the most important of scenes, and is at the mercy of the men. Though this is the case, Cook believes her to be a figure of true power within the play who all men seem to fear. She states that "...it is often silent Hero who figures the threat..." (Cook 190). This is a baseless stance as Hero provides no evidence of being superior in any sort of fashion. Carol Cook's defense of this statement is that

25

Hero is in the position to turn Claudio into a cuckold. That is, she has the ability to cheat on Claudio and embarrass him. Though this statement is undoubted, it fails to move Hero into a position of power. In theory, Claudio is also able to cheat on Hero and embarrass her as well. Furthermore, Hero hardly retains any sort of powerful traits due to her position. What truly matters when making bold statements about power and control is evidence. With that being said, Carol Cook's reasoning is weightless as the men in Hero's life have absolute control over her. For example, Claudio expects her to marry him even though, "Obviously she is not much in love with Claudio, whom she barely knows..." (King 146). According to King, Claudio's desire to have and own Hero tells a more, "...monetary story" (King 147). In the first act of the play, Claudio asks Benedick, "Can the world buy such a jewel?" (Shakespeare 9). This question displays how Hero is an object to Claudio. Given the way Hero lets herself be treated by Claudio, the love story becomes very mechanical, cold, and impersonal. In addition, besides her father, she is able to be controlled by other men as well, and this is witnessed when, "...Don Pedro makes up the match between Hero and Claudio..." (Lewalski 238). She is also taken aside and led around by Don Pedro after he asks her, "With me in your company?" (Shakespeare 21). From the friar to Leonato, and from Don Pedro to Claudio, the men hold the power to command the powerless Hero.

Though she does not physically exist, the weakest female character in the play is Hero's imaginary cousin. While the character only exists in the mind, she is important to discuss as she reveals quite a bit about the structure of power within the play. Leonato's imaginary niece makes her first appearance after the feigned death of Hero. Leonato commands Claudio to marry his niece, or Hero's cousin, to make up for the incident involving Hero. Moreover, she is given away without her consent. This event occurs in the fifth act when Leonato states, "My brother hath a daughter, almost a copy of my child..." (Shakespare 89). The imaginary cousin is never asked if she would enjoy being married to Claudio, and is instead handed to Claudio.

26

Within an instant, a wedding is arranged, and the cousin is given to Claudio as if she is an object. In addition, this imaginary cousin is far weaker than Hero as she does not have a voice. While it is true that Hero is barely able to state her mind, her imaginary cousin is without any words up until the wedding ceremony. She is without any influence, and has no ability to act, command or control. In the simplest of terms, Hero's cousin is merely there. Ranking far below all other women of the play, Hero's imaginary cousin is an important figure, because she has absolutely no power. She is the embodiment of all that is wrong with a patriarchal society, objectification, and social constraints.

Though most of the men seem to be figures of authority, Leonato is undoubtedly the most powerful of the group. Though Don Pedro is nobility, Leonato is the unchallenged ruler of the house, and nobody fails to comply with him. This renders him as being the primary figure of authority in the play. Additionally, he is able to command everyone, both female and male. He offers advice to Beatrice, speaks harshly towards Claudio and Don Pedro, and even commands Claudio to marry his imaginary niece. An example of his advice to Beatrice comes in the second act as he says, "Well, niece, I hope to see you one day fitted with a husband" (Shakespeare 20). As a result of these actions, it is clear that Leonato is not only the most powerful male in the play, but the most powerful character.

Claudio is the second most powerful male character, and one of the most powerful people within the play. Carol Cook explains that Claudio is actually weak, because he is more feminine than the other men in the play. He is, if Cook is to be believed, a weak and paranoid individual. She also acknowledges that Claudio is in a vulnerable position as, "Hero is the focus of masculine anxieties" (Cook 190). Furthermore, Claudio, in his love for Hero, sets himself up to be damaged. Carol Cook further supports her theory by stating that marriage sets men up for humiliation (Cook 187). This is not just the case with Claudio and Hero, but is the case for anyone who becomes involved in a relationship. Therefore, the same could be said for Hero as she may be setting herself up for humiliation. Perhaps Claudio will eventually cheat on her, embarrassing her in the process. Carol Cook's explanations of Claudio's weakness are themselves weak, and are not strengthened with evidence from the text. In truth, Claudio is highly powerful. An example of his power would be when he sees Hero, and must have her. In the first act of the play, he states, "In mine eye she is the sweetest lady that ever I looked on" (Shakespeare 9) He never has the chance to explore Hero's personality, but instead simply loves her at first sight. She is a beautiful object, and he must have her for himself. Further evidence of Claudio's power over women comes when he labels Hero as a jewel that must be bought. To sum up, she is a purchasable figure of beauty to Claudio, and is far weaker than him. Hero is in no way more powerful than Claudio as she never commands him, allows herself to be treated as an object, and holds no authority over him.

Though Claudio is in a position of power, there is one key weakness that plagues him. The primary issue in the play, Hero sleeping with another man, is put into full swing as, "Claudio is certain he saw her entertaining another man..." (Simonds 411). Unfortunately, this whole event damages Claudio's power within the play. Sadly, he does not begin to question the rumors, but instead asks, "Disloyal?" (Shakespeare 51). Don John's ability to manipulate, and Claudio's inability to resist said manipulations expose Claudio's primary weakness. He lets himself be fully absorbed into Don John's lie, and is without a mind of his own to process the hurtful event. Nova Myhill states in "Spectatorship in/of *Much Ado About Nothing*" that Claudio's, "...eyes are extensions of Don John's vision, not [his] own" (Myhill 292). Without the occurrence of this weakening event, Claudio would not have any significant weaknesses. Even so, he still remains a very powerful character, and holds much more power than any of the women in the play.

With Benedick's level of power within the play ranking closely to Beatrice's, he is by far the weakest male character. Although he is the weakest, he would like others to believe him to be strong. Stephen B. Dobranski reinforces this idea in his article "Children of the Mind: Miscarried

28

Narratives in *Much Ado About Nothing*" by stating that "Benedick allies himself with Hercules by comparing Beatrice to Omphale" (Dobranski 235). Furthermore, Benedick's lack of power stems from his inability to marry a woman, and his inability to resist the commands of Beatrice. When Beatrice commands him to "kill Claudio," he hesitates only for a brief moment, and heads off to complete his assigned objective (Shakespeare 74). The gravity of the situation is alarming as he, "...agrees to challenge his best friend to a mortal duel" (Simonds 412). No other man in the play is commanded so easily, let alone commanded. In a period of time where men held all of the power, his almost instant agreement to kill Claudio on behalf of Beatrice is shocking. In addition, Benedick's weakness is further displayed as he is far too paranoid of women's power through marriage. He makes it very clear that he is, "...strongly against romance and marriage" (Henze 188). In the first act of the play, Benedick explains, "...for I truly love none" (Shakespeare 7). Carol Cook explains his fear in stating that "To submit oneself to a woman by loving and marrying her [is] announcing one's humiliation to the world" (Cook 189). Given the time period, he should be more willing to cast his fears of feminine power aside, and find a woman to marry. Instead, he lets himself be consumed by said fears of the woman becoming, "...doubly threatening..." (Cook 189). As Carol Cook writes, Benedick is host to, "...anxiety about women's potential power over men..." (Cook 189). Interestingly, Carl Dennis, author of "Wit and Wisdom in *Much Ado About Nothing*," believes Benedick actually longs to get married from the start. He explains that, in the beginning of the play, Benedick's, "...case of self-deception is also dramatized by his vexation at Claudio's immediately falling in love with Hero" (Dennis 225). It is clear that Benedick would like to be married, but he cannot get over his fears of female power. In conclusion, though he is a man in a patriarchal society, and Beatrice must rely on him to kill Claudio, his power is nowhere near that of other men. In comparison to Leonato and Claudio, Benedick fails to equally match up. While he is more powerful than Hero and her imaginary cousin, Benedick proves himself to be the weakest of the male characters.

All female characters in *Much Ado About Nothing*, except Beatrice, hold no real power, leaving it for most of the men. With the exception of Benedick, the men of the play have the ability to make commands, control others and influence people. For example, Claudio is able to freely pick a wife among the women, and demand that she marries him. Once the said wedding is demanded, Leonato arranges it without the approval of his weak daughter, Hero. Moreover, these actions set the tone for the entire play as the women are weak and without any power, closely resembling objects rather than actual people.

SOURCES

Babula, William. ""Much Ado about Nothing" and the Spectator." *South Atlantic Bulletin* 41.1 (1976): 9-15. *JSTOR*. Web. 17 Sep. 2009.

Cook, Carol. "The Sign and Semblance of Her Honor." *Modern Language Association* 101.2 (1986): 186-202. *JSTOR*. Web. 18 Aug. 2009.

Dennis, Carl. "Wit and Wisdom in *Much Ado about Nothing*." *Studies in English Literature, 1500-1900* 13.2 (1973): 223-237. *JSTOR*. Web. 17 Sep. 2009.

Dobranski, Stephen B. "Children of the Mind: Miscarried Narratives in *Much Ado about* Nothing." *Studies in English Literature, 1500-1900* 38.2 (1998): 233-250. *JSTOR*. Web. 17 Sep. 2009.

Henze, Richard. "Deception in *Much Ado about Nothing*." *Studies in English Literature, 1500*-1900 11.2 (1971): 187-201. *JSTOR*. Web. 17 Sep. 2009.

King, Walter N. "Much Ado About Something." *Shakespeare Quarterly* 15.3 (1964): 143-155. *JSTOR*. Web. 17 Sep. 2009.

Lewalski, B. K. "Love, Appearance and Reality: Much Ado about Something." *Studies in* English Literature, 1500-1900 8.2 (1968): 235-251. *JSTOR*. Web. 17 Sep. 2009.

Myhill, Nova. "Spectatorship in/of "Much Ado about Nothing."" *Studies in English Literature, 1500-1900* 39.2 (1999): 291-311. *JSTOR*. Web. 17 Sep. 2009

Shakespeare, William. *Much Ado About Nothing*. Ed. David L. Stevenson. New York: New American Library, 1998. 3-101.

Simonds, Munoz. "Much Ado About Nothing." *Educational Theatre Review* 29.3 (1977): 411-412. *JSTOR*. Web. 17 Sep. 2009.

4. Damned if He Does, Damned if He Doesn't: A look at Chaucer's portrayal of women in *The Canterbury Tales*

The Interpretation of Man

When examining the literary criticism of Chaucer's *The Canterbury Tales*, critics have presented supportive evidence that reinforces two contrasting ideas: that Chaucer may have been pro feminist, or that he may not have been. On one hand, he does tend to portray women as unruly, daring and provocative figures. On the other hand, the women of his writings can be identified as early feminist figures. Other critics take different approaches, believing that authorial intention may have been lost over the last several hundred years, rendering the text far too ambiguous to define. Edwin D. Crawn uses a unique approach, stressing that what Chaucer wrote was confined by the historical norms found in literature. Furthermore, these alternative approaches to Chaucer's writing must be investigated further. Pursuing the relationship between history and literature may prove to give modern readers a better understanding of why Chaucer wrote the way he did on feminism. With evidence to support both sides, both arguments must be explored in depth in order to reach a more definite conclusion, one that conclusively states whether or not Chaucer was for or against feminism.

First, in attempting to adequately explore both sides of Chaucer's writing, many critics who lean towards his texts being pro women must be examined. In "Chaucer's Wife of Bath, Hoccleve's Arguing Women, and Lydgate's Herford Wives," written by Heather Hill-Vasquez, the female characters within *The Canterbury Tales* are seen as being early feminist figures. According to Hill-Vasquez, Chaucer uses the Wife of Bath as a vehicle to broadcast a message of pro feminism. For example, Alison is an unusually exceptional female character whose intelligence is superior to that of many men. Hill-Vasquez explains how, "...it is Alison's independently minded interpretations of theological texts and doctrines that are central to her apparent embodiment of female rebellion..." (Hill-Vasquez 173). In other words, her role as a skillful interpreter is so unusual, that she is seen in more of a negative light as opposed to positive. Furthermore, Hill-Vasquez states that Alison is, "...an energetic interpreter who feels free to explore theological texts and intuit their meanings, even if they appear to conflict with what male authorities have asserted." (Hill-Vasquez 174). Given the time period in which Chaucer wrote *The Canterbury Tales*, such a female character is just as surprising as she is inspiring. In addition, Hill-Vasquez stresses that Alison is, "...meant as an interpreting woman" (Hill-Vasquez 176). The primary element to Alison as an early feminist icon is her ability to interpret, and Hill-Vasquez feels as if it is a, "...fundamentally positive [element] of the figure" (Hill-Vasquez 174). Also discussed briefly is Chaucer's *Wife of Bath's Tale*. Both Alison and the Wife of Bath share the praise, with the latter undoubtedly possessing, "...interpretive ingenuity..." (Hill-Vasquez 185). Moreover, the Wife of Bath's actions are interpreted as being even greater than Alison's, because of, "...the association of her actions with the beneficent, redemptive work of the Virgin Mary..." (Hill-Vasquez 185). The actions and characteristics of said women are so helpful, that they, "...could perhaps be indulged, tolerated, [and] even embraced..." (Hill-Vasquez 185). While some critics of *The Canterbury Tales* tend to steer clear of drawing lines and making definitive statements about Chaucer's stance on feminism, Hill-Vasquez does not. She makes it absolutely clear that Chaucer was most likely for feminism, and the Wife of Bath and Alison are her evidence.

Al Walzem also takes a firm stance on Chaucer's positive view of feminism in "Peynted by the Lion: The Wife of Bath as Feminist Pedagogue." Walzem feels as if there cannot be ambiguity in the *Wife of Bath's Tale*, but instead that Chaucer uses the Wife of Bath as a tool to help women. He notes how, "The Wife of Bath ... does not seem to be like other women" (Walzem 45). She is not quiet and timid, but is instead talkative and active. Surprisingly, she is able to freely speak her mind in the company of other men, which is an uncommon trait for women of the time. As for Alison, Walzem explains that she, "...is rich, confident, and unafraid to leave the domestic sphere and travel freely, not only about England but even as far as Jerusalem" (Walzem 47). Additionally, Walzem takes interest in how, "...she is apparently a good and competent businesswoman" (Walzem 47). Oddly enough, with all of her traits considered, Alison appears to be more masculine than feminine. She is so open and powerful that she seems distanced from most other women. Most women of the time were quiet, timid and stayed in the background, but, "...she makes no attempt to bury her past and put on a more modest, "appropriate" front. Instead [she] coarsely advertises the seamier aspects of her past..." (Walzem 49). According to Walzem, the Wife of Bath does not appear to be stereotypical or poor representations of women. Rather, they, with the help of Chaucer's writing, are figures of feminist progress and power. On the contrary, some critics feel as if this is not the case at all, and have evidence to support their claims.

In Elizabeth Scala's "Desire in the Canterbury Tales: Sovereignty and Mastery Between the Wife and Clerk," she focuses on the negative aspects of the *Wife of Bath's Tale*. She feels that "The Wife makes feminine desire her explicit subject..." (Scala 83). As opposed to being an early feminist figure who pushes for women's rights, the Wife of Bath comes across as a damaging figure. Additionally, Scala points out how the Wife of Bath is able to make, "... diverse arguments for the necessity of female dominance..." but is unable to stick to her stance by the end of her segment. Unfortunately, even though she is able to rise up and speak her mind, "...she withdraws back into belligerence in the space of a mere eight lines" (Scala 86). Scala understands her retreat within those eight lines to be indicative of Chaucer's inability to commit to feminism. Even though he gave her a powerful voice for most of her prologue and tale, he himself retreats, leaving his writing to be more damaging than it is helpful. For as damaging as Scala's criticism of the *Wife of Bath's Tale* is, some critics view Chaucer in a far worse light.

Perhaps the most negative of the reviews written within the last few

33

years, "Contested Authority: Jerome and the Wife of Bath on I Timothy 2," written by Theresa Tinkle, casts Chaucer in a strongly antifeminist light. Focusing on the history of the time, Tinkle states, "The Wife of Bath enters history in the midst of unresolved controversies over the relation of the laity, and particularly women, to Scripture" (Tinkle 284). With that being said, it makes perfect sense that Chaucer would have her delivering, "...a literate antimatrimonial "sermon," replete with scriptural citations and translations..." (Tinkle 284). Chaucer attempts to start the Wife of Bath off on a bad foot, allowing her to be both provocative and daring by using scripture to support her argument. Moreover, Chaucer takes it one step further by allowing her to reject, "...both spousal and apostolic authority..." in her sermon (Tinkle 284). Without a doubt, the Wife of Bath is rebellious and daring, but these actions failed to impress some readers. Also, Tinkle believes that Chaucer fails in his bigotry to a certain degree, because more complex arguments are replaced, "...with simplified, more comfortable gender conflicts" (Tinkle 291). In other words, even though Chaucer targets women and portrays them as being unruly, he is unable to do it well. His best attempts at doing so are mere pokes at lightweight gender conflicts. Unfortunately for both sides of the debate, many modern literary critics feel that Chaucer's writing cannot be so easily defined.

In Mark David Rasmussen's "Feminist Chaucer? Some Implications for Teaching," he brings up several issues within *The Canterbury Tales* that may damage the arguments of both sides. Focusing on the Wife of Bath, Rasmussen believes that she provides for many instances where female stereotypes are both reinforced and broken down. In support for Chaucer pointing out the absurdity of stereotypes, he explains that, "Through her, then, Chaucer represents a stereotypical image of women in order to show how that stereotype imprisons and confines" (Rasmussen 78). If Chaucer's *Wife of Bath's Tale* is to be read this way, he appears to be helpful as the text is explanatory. However, Rasmussen also cautions that there are, "Two very different views, then, of Chaucer and his relation to women (Rasmussen 80).

As opposed to being a misogynist, Chaucer could instead be seen as an early feminist. For example, Rasmussen explains how, "This interpretation of the Wife as both reflecting and reflecting upon antifeminist commonplaces is largely persuasive..." (Rasmussen 78). In other words, it is not difficult to believe he uses the Wife of Bath as an early feminist tool, because she serves so many purposes. Furthermore, the Wife of Bath practices a rebelliousness not often seen in medieval times, and even tends to fit the standard portrait of a woman by being both chatty and skillful with fabrics. Rasmussen feels as if, "Writing the truth of woman's existence . . . means not turning one's back on stereotypes, but accepting that their existence is the centrally important and interesting fact to be confronted" (Rasmussen 79). If this reading of the text is preferred, and Chaucer did confront these stereotypes head on, it still remains a mystery as to how much his efforts helped. Oddly enough, "...medieval constructions of gender strike students as both foreign and uncomfortably familiar..." (Rasmussen 82). In conclusion, as opposed to taking a side as to whether Chaucer was a bigot playing off of the damaging stereotypes of women or just an author illustrating the absurdity of stereotyping, Rasmussen leaves it up to ambiguity. This non-western approach to Chaucer's writing is seldom witnessed, but holds a great deal of strength. Perhaps, as the title suggests, the question of Chaucer being a feminist is one left impossible to answer as there are two opposite readings, both of which with significant evidence and support.

Gregory M. Sadlek's "Chaucer in the Dock: Literature, Women, and Medieval Antifeminism" continues the investigation of ambiguity in Chaucer's texts. He explains how, "...Chaucer's relationship to women is still a critical issue" (Sadlek 117). The issue is still highly debated, largely due to both sides having evidence to support their argument. On one hand, Sadlek feels as if, "...Chaucer wrote in the context of deep-seated misogyny" (Sadlek 117). For example, the Wife of Bath appears to be a stereotypical woman. However, on the other hand, Chaucer seems to have a, "...continual interest in women..." and may show this through, "...his complex and apparently sympathetic portrayal of women characters..." (Sadlek 118). As mentioned earlier, perhaps Chaucer's goal is actually to address women's issues by exposing the audience to them. By confronting these issues, "Chaucer is clearly woman's friend and an inventive critic of the male patriarchy" (Sadlek 118). Unfortunately for critics who believe Chaucer is strictly for or against feminism, Sadlek takes his approach in a third direction by focusing on ambiguity. Perhaps Chaucer himself cannot be defined by what he writes, no matter how supportive or offensive. Sadlek explains that "...the voices of Chaucer's characters cannot necessarily be equated with that of Chaucer himself" (Sadlek 123). Furthermore, Sadlek feels, "...even if a Chaucerian character speaks antifeminist rhetoric, readers may not be able to use that text to prove conclusively that Chaucer himself was antifeminist" (Sadlek 123). In other words, even though there are two approaches to Chaucer's female characters, pinpointing his stance on feminism cannot be done through a close reading of the text. Sadlek feels as if Chaucer's beliefs cannot be defined by interpreting what he writes, no matter how well both sides are presented.

Dean Swinford appears to further Sadlek's take on Chaucer in his article "Transforming the Trickster in Chaucer's *Wife of Bath's Tale*." Relying solely on text from the *Wife of Bath's Tale*, Swinford is able to construct an argument for both sides. First, Chaucer does appear to be, "...presenting a take on the "war of the sexes..." (Swinford 230). Swinford feels that the text shows how Chaucer is not standing on the sidelines, but is instead injecting his own opinion into the text. Additionally, Swinford finds that the, "...reference to her skill in weaving may be intended to undercut her authority" (Swinford 232). However, as Sadlek points out, Chaucer also appears to be using the Wife of Bath as a tool to criticize the men of his time. In sum, with Chaucer appearing to be both pro and antifeminist, there can be no definitive understanding of his stance on feminism. Swinford notes how, "Scholars have attempted to uncover Chaucer's complex views on gender and the power struggles that ensue in relationships, but they have been unable to conclusively prove..." nearly anything (Swinford 231). After the supporting and contrasting evidence for both sides of the debate are analyzed, Swinford feels as if Chaucer may not have wanted to take a side in this debate, but instead merely stay perfectly in the middle. While literary critics have made their cases for Chaucer being pro or antifeminist, both, or neither, some take the approach to the *Wife of Bath's Tale* in a completely different direction.

Almost fully removing itself from the debate, the most surprising approach to Chaucer's writing is historically based. "Allas, Allas! That Evere Love Was Synne: Excuses For Sin and the Wife of Bath's Stars" by Edwin D. Crawn takes a different approach altogether to Chaucer's stance on women. He feels as if Chaucer's view of feminism may be misunderstood by modern audiences, because it was more of a historical issue. Even though the, "...Wife of Bath presents herself in her prologue by exploiting the commonplaces of authoritative clerical discourse: biblical exegesis, marriage sermons, treatises on virginity, and misogamous satire" there may be a more simple reason for her actions (Crawn 33). In the several hundred years since Chaucer wrote *The Canterbury Tales*, everything has changed from politics to literary conventions. Crawn explains how, in the time of Chaucer, it was common to have characters giving lengthy confessions. Though it may not appear to be a confession at first glance, it does allow for the Wife of Bath to clear her conscience of her sins. He writes that "Excusing sin or defending sin ... became itself a topos in pastoral discourse on sin and confession, coming to the fore as the clergy ... worked to create informed confessions and informed penitents" (Crawn 34). Moreover, it is important to note that "This style of literature flourished especially in England, where..." the clergy pushed for confession (Crawn 34). In other words, Chaucer's stance on women may not even be present in the Wife of Bath's story. Instead, he could have merely been writing in a popular style for his English audience. Therefore, if there is anything Chaucer can be judged for in this text, it is that this kind of literature, "...gave [people] alternative ways of reading their own lives..." (Crawn 34). People could talk about their sins, indirectly confessing for them in the process, and carry on with their lives as if they had never sinned at all. Out of the approaches examined, Crawn's does an amazing job of shedding new light on the topic of Chaucer's possible stance on feminism.

Contemporary conventions in literature have shed new light on the age old debate of whether or not Chaucer was for or against feminism. Before recent times, most critics took one side of the argument and presented large amounts of evidence to support their claims. However, this trend is slowly declining as many critics are now seeing the futility in such a debate. With both sides being able to support their arguments, it is thought that the text may be too ambiguous to accurately define. Perhaps the *Wife of Bath's Tale* is purposely ambiguous, allowing for Chaucer to have fun by picking on women and also get serious by criticizing men. There is also the possibility that everyone could be missing the point, as Edwin D. Crawn stresses, and that Chaucer was merely following the trends of Middle Ages literature. Furthermore, dissecting the ambiguity of the text may prove to be useful in finding a acceptable conclusion to the debate. Further exploring the ambiguousness of Chaucer's *Wife of Bath's Tale* has its strengths and weaknesses. On one hand, many critics' arguments will be rendered ineffective and exhaustive as their firm stances on Chaucer's views are actually futile. On the other hand, pursuing this avenue will allow for modern day critics to explore contemporary issues such as whether this ambiguity is purposeful or unintentional. In conclusion, even though a few critics above have stressed it is difficult for either stance can be argued in full, not doing so leaves a massive gap where a conclusion could fit in. Such a conclusion can be determined only after examining several scholarly sources in which the author does make a definitive statement about Chaucer's stance on feminism.

After an initial examination of recent scholarship on Chaucer, his relationship to feminism must be pursued further in order to better understand the issue. Despite the first scan of criticisms resulting in ambiguity, this result can be investigated deeper in order to find a more conclusive answer. In the early research, it seemed as if the case was clearly made for Chaucer being both a feminist and an anti-feminist. While on one hand he appears to do women a favor in his writings, strengthening them in his stories, he also appears to push stereotypes which result in a damaged image. Moving onward, in order to better understand Chaucer's writing and potential motives, it is important to investigate the literary customs and atmosphere of the medieval period.

Similar to the authors of today, the authors of medieval Europe often times borrowed and shared ideas from one another. While it is largely debatable whether or not Chaucer read various other authors' works, it is known that he does share similar views and writing styles with others. Martha Driver's "Romancing the *Rose*: The Readings of Chaucer and Christine" explores the idea that Chaucer was not alone in his writings, as others appeared to be like-minded. Driver notes that, "Geoffrey Chaucer [draws] on a common stock of stories that circulated in England and on the Continent..." (Driver 147). With so many of the same ideas drifting about a civilized and educated culture, it is to be expected that authors begin to share, even if done so unknowingly. Driver further explains how writers, "read and were influenced by many of the same authors..." (Driver 148). For example, it is theorized that Chaucer's writings are similar in style to those of Christine de Pizan, yet it is thought that he may have never actually read any of her works. On the other hand, he could have read her works and other works from afar, because he, "read French..." (Driver 149). In other words, whether done so indirectly or directly, authors often share and borrow ideas from others. What this explanation of borrowing intends to explain is that authors often write about safe topics. After looking at the broad spectrum of medieval writers and how they share topics, it is entirely plausible that Chaucer was writing negatively about women. Given the status of women at the time, his supposedly comical attitude could instead be one expressing the seriousness in his criticisms. On the contrary, it is fitting that his portrayal of women was just his way of poking fun at women, playing around with the stereotypes present at the time. Moving onward, it is best to take a glance at the environment in which Chaucer was writing as it may help the reader to comprehend the atmosphere in which he was writing.

A better understanding of the atmosphere Chaucer was writing in is made possible by broadly examining the medieval literary environment. Nancy Partner's article titled "Studying Medieval Women: Sex, Gender, Feminism" investigates to what degree the era may have or have not been accepting to women. She explains, "*Studying Medieval Women* opens with Judith Bennett's historical survey and assessment of the status of women scholars in academe and the Medieval Academy, and of feminist scholarship in the medieval fields" (Partner 306). Her explanation proves surprising as the idea of woman scholars in a time as misogynistic as the middle ages seems unrealistic, especially after a brief overview of common stereotypes. Continuing the investigation, "Carol Glover examines early Scandinavian laws and sagas for evidence of the precise nature of their unstated assumptions about sex and gender..." (Partner 307). Not surprisingly, "she finds that gender, organized around an exacting ideal of masculinity, was a system of values only loosely connected to maleness or femaleness" (Partner 307). Therefore, what was masculine was to be taken seriously and respected, and what was feminine was to be placed in a subordinate position. Intriguingly enough, she found information suggesting that it is, "better a son who is your daughter than no son at all." With that being said, the status of women at the time, especially outside of England, was quite low. This idea is concreted by the previous statement of a homosexual son even being superior than that of a daughter. Lastly, Partner explains that this investigation was an attempt to get a, "coherent picture of medieval culture..." (Partner 307). While she does not explain anything revolutionary in terms of misogyny or sexism, she does illustrate the sort of world in which Chaucer was writing. It is thought that this proposed world must have been full of female readers, with many of them adoring Chaucer's style.

It is thought that Chaucer may not have been writing for a broader

40

crowd, but rather for a female audience. Joyce Boro, author of "John Fletcher's *Women Pleased* and the Pedagogy of Reading Romance," explains how Chaucer may have been writing to appeal to more feminine readers. It is no wonder *The Wife of Bath's Tale* has stood the test of time with it being even more popular today than it was when Chaucer penned it. Featured a countless number of times in academia, critics have noted how it is, "highly ambiguous and popular..." (Boro 188). Ambiguity, or the presence of several plausible understandings with credible evidence to defend them, is an issue in *The Wife of Bath's Tale*. Of the many literary critics to examine the text, many appear to be split on deciding whether or not Chaucer was a feminist writer. Furthermore, Boro ponders the question herself, explaining how there is a tendency, "of the romance genre to ascribe power to female utterances" (Boro 188). She wonders further, but decides that "regardless of who read romances or why, it is incontestable that the genre was gendered as feminine and that it offered a recognizable imaginative space of female agency..." (Boro 190). In other words, the debate on whether or not this sort of text is geared towards women is, according to Boro, a debate no longer. Perhaps Chaucer knew women would be reading his material in massive quantities, thus explaining the Wife of Bath's characteristics. In addition, Boro states how, "The Wife of Bath's pronouncements on female sovereignty were well known..." (Boro 191). Even though it was understood just how powerful and symbolic the Wife of Bath was when her story was written, Boro fears that not much has changed since then. Looking back, it seems as if, "the Wife of Bath's tactics suggest that despite the passage of time ... the formal debate has not advanced the female cause" (Boro 196). With that being said, it is still important to understand the Wife of Bath's significance, especially given the time period in which *The Canterbury Tales* were written. Also, while Chaucer's best effort to write in favor of women did not drastically change anything, Boro feels as if, "it suggests that literature is a more successful venue in which to advance the female cause..." (Boro 196). In conclusion, Boro feels that Chaucer must have been writing in favor of women. If not for his genuine appreciation of the gender, then for the sake of pleasing his overwhelmingly female audience. However, while this position may be held by Boro, other scholars more firmly believe that Chaucer had good intentions that yielded bad results.

Investigating stereotypes and anti-feminism, Elaine Treharne looks at who is writing the reviews and what Chaucer's writings actually means for women. She begins by explaining her opinion that most, "unfavourable readings are by male critics." (Treharne 94). She feels that even within the criticism of this already sexist text is simply more sexism. Also, while Chaucer attempts, "to emulate aspects of a woman's language," he unfortunately does it, "from an entirely stereotypically conceived basis" (Treharne 96). In other words, even Chaucer's attempt to give women a voice is a feeble one, resulting not in empowerment, but rather the use of more of the same old stereotypes. Almost humorously, Treharne explains, "Although Chaucer himself has been regarded by some scholars as a proto-feminist writer, this seems akin to anachronistic wishful thinking" (Treharne 100). Treharne intends to separate truth from fiction, explaining that he is not the feminist writer some believe him to be. While, of course, "he is a writer whose fictional creations deliberately raise issues of the relationship between language and social structures," these actions actually end up damaging not just the perceptions of the characters, but the feminist movement as well (Treharne 100). She firmly believes, "male authors like Chaucer actually [weaken] the Wife's position, and [stereotype] her even as she tries to throw the anti-feminist stereotyping book back at her husbands" (Treharne 104). Therefore, what Treharne believes is that Chaucer may have had good intentions, but it is unlikely. Also, she feels as if any good intentions he had were immediately wasted as he relies on stereotypes to make his point. In return, he does little or nothing other than strengthen the stereotypes he may be attempting to end. Yet, according to some scholars, this may be a result of his poor education on the opposite sex.

Rachel Ann Baumgardner takes an interesting approach to Chaucer, pondering if it is his lack of knowledge that may have tainted the character. Immediately in her article titled "I Alisoun, I Wife: Foucault's Three Egos and the *Wife of Bath's Prologue*," she notes that the events seen in *The Wife of Bath's Tale* remind, "the audience that the "Wife" is, in fact, as fictive creation of Geoffrey Chaucer, a man with little or no empathetic knowledge of women" (Baumgardner 2). This statement means that, while his intentions may be that of good, he is unable to execute properly and fully as his knowledge of women and their status is rusty. Whether it is done unknowingly or not, Baumgardner feels as if the story actually, "describes how Chaucer condescends to his creation..." (Baumgardner 2). She furthers her statement by explaining, "though possibly unintentional or even subconscious, this language that establishes a hierarchy in the text appears throughout feminist criticism" (Baumgardner 2). In other words, whether he means to or not, he ends up creating a position of inferiority for the female characters in his text. Additionally, Baumgardner arrives at a crossroads partway through her article, each route equally as luring. She states that "the Wife of Bath's inability to speak for herself leave feminist scholars with a dilemma" (Baumgardner 3). It is difficult to determine exactly how to judge the Wife of Bath as a character. On one hand, "to disregard completely the Wife of Bath's importance as an energetic, engaging, and ultimately female voice would undermine the significance of the issues that she raises, especially within her *Prologue*" (Baumgardner 3). While Chaucer does do an excellent job of portraying her as a stereotypical woman, there are simply too many strengths to ignore. Yet, on the other hand, "how ... does one highlight the importance of the Wife of Bath as both a character and a speaker while still recognizing [she's] an invention of Geoffrey Chaucer?" (Baumgardner 3). This resulting ambiguity is troubling if looking for a definitively positive answer, because both sides of the argument are plausible and have strong evidence. At her article's end, Baumgardner finds it difficult to determine whether or not the Wife of Bath is to be seen as a positive, strengthening figure, or a stereotypically weak figure created by a poorly educated Chaucer. As for other scholars, it is thought that Chaucer was actually in the opposite position, intending to be negative and only seeming positive on accident.

While still agreeing that Chaucer was an anti-feminist, Shawn Normandin takes a far different approach to *The Canterbury Tales*. In his article, titled "The Wife of Bath's Urinary Imagination," he feels as if Chaucer intends to portray her as disgusting, often pushing scatological imagery when having her speak or be described. He explains how, "the urine in her prologue thus makes the Wife vulnerable to misogynistic interpretation" (Normandin 244). While the vileness of her story may first appear to damage her image, Normandin states that her better traits shine through. He believes that "the Wife of Bath is a rhetorician of great skill" (Normandin 247). Instead of focusing on the often putrid words and activities Chaucer uses, he instead focuses on the Wife of Bath's strengths. Furthermore, what's more important to him is, "the Wife's struggle to avoid the silence men would impose on her" (Normandin 251). While the scatological imagery used by Chaucer is believed by Normandin to be an attempt to make the Wife of Bath, as well as all other women, look bad, it is not simply an invitation to misogynists. Instead, it allows her strengths to shine through for the audience. According to Normandin, Chaucer may have been writing negatively about the Wife of Bath, but his plan backfires as it only serves to help her in the long run. Others share his understanding of the text, finding that, no matter what her portrayal in the text, she is a positive figure for feminists. After researching criticisms that focus on the middle ages and earlier interpretations of the text, it is crucial to shift gears and examine Chaucer's writings in relation to today.

Maria O'Neill partially examines *The Wife of Bath's Tale* through a new historicist lens, comparing the text's criticisms with today's norms. She opens her article titled "Gender, Economics and Morality: Sexuality and Aging as Depicted in Geoffrey Chaucer's *The Canterbury Tales*" by stating, "Nowadays, middle aged or elderly women who embark on relations of a sexual or dubious nature with younger men are a cause for opprobrium, targets of media moralizing and nudge-and-wink gossip" (O'Neill 73).

Meaning, if what Chaucer wrote were to happen today, the result would surely be a maelstrom of media attention. Almost overnight, she would be the hot topic, found in news papers, magazines and television shows. With that being said, she explains how, "...these women are stereotyped either as victims of go-getting instant fame seekers or as insatiable sexual pariahs, preying on hirsute young men whose mole-like libido surfaces blindly every so often" (O'Neill 73). In other words, while opinions of sexually promiscuous females are debatable in our contemporary society, they were certainly not in the medieval period. When Chaucer writes about her suspicious and outright odd relationships, there is a good chance he knows what will be the audience's reaction. Additionally, O'Neill feels as if, even though reactions would be negative, Chaucer wrote the way he did on purpose. For example, she feels that "Young maids and married women were by Chaucer's rule of thumb allowed to be coy, unfaithful, sexual incontinent, deceitful and skittish" (O'Neill 74). For him, these characteristics possibly seemed to fit the Wife of Bath, allowing for Chaucer to paint what he believed to be a fitting picture of the character. In addition, O'Neill breaks away from modern interpretations to simply examine the Wife of Bath for who she is, and what she means for women. O'Neill states that "Her dynamism and foresight give, perhaps in spite of Chaucer's original intentions, [provide] an attractive portrait of the mature woman" (O'Neill 74). In other words, despite Chaucer's attempt at negatively portraying the Wife of Bath, he fails as she seems to be much deeper and intriguing than originally intended.

Antonina Harbus examines the text in a similar fashion to O'Neill, and also arrives at a negative conclusion. Unlike other literary critics who examine *The Canterbury Tales* from a medieval point of view, she also attempts to put the text under a new historicist lens. Harbus' "Interpreting *The Wife of Bath's Prologue* and *Tale* in a Contemporary Note to Thynne's 1532 Edition" looks at the Wife of Bath's treatment, as well as her overall characteristics. Firstly, she makes a quick note of how Chaucer's character, "objects to the orthodox gender roles indicated in the text..." (Harbus 6). She

45

claims that Chaucer may be hurting the feminist cause, and cheaply relies on, "the extremely negative claims put into the mouth of the Wife of Bath" (Harbus 6). In other words, though Chaucer seems to be making the Wife of Bath into a positively helpful character, he is actually turning her into something far worse. In addition to seeming negative and mean spirited, Harbus also believes Chaucer does misogynists a favor by allowing her to speak so freely about gender. She explains how he reinforces, "the contemporaneous popular idea of the Wife of Bath as an unreliable commentator on sexual politics" (Harbus 7). Even though her rants and complaints appear to be vocally freeing and empowering, Harbus feels as if this is not Chaucer's intent. When examining her words and actions today, it appears as if he must have been working against women.

After reviewing numerous sources in order to better understand Chaucer's writings and intentions, it seemed as if ambiguity was the end result. Perhaps there were no concrete answers to the question of whether or not Chaucer was indeed an anti-feminist. It seemed as if he rested safely in the middle, in a gray area where multiple conclusions could be defended with credible evidence. However, after arriving at said conclusion, ambiguity was unacceptable as a destination and began to serve as a motivation to research further. Furthermore, researching and examining the scholarship provided for articles written by Partner and Driver, who explained the literary atmosphere and stressed that Chaucer wrote similarly to others, respectively. In addition, Boro was one of few scholars to cast Chaucer in a wholly positive light, stating that he was writing for his female audience. However, she is one of few to find him as a positive figure. For example, Treharne finds his use of stereotypes to be damaging, and Baumgardner feels as if he is simply too poorly educated on women in order to even portray them accurately. Normandin and O'Neill differ from others, finding that he attempts to cast the Wife of Bath in a negative light only to have his intentions backfire. Instead, they note that the negative imagery only serves to highlight her better traits. Lastly, both O'Neill and Harbus examine *The Canterbury Tales* from a new historicist point of view, finding that even today Chaucer's writings appear to depict women as negative figures. As a result, it would seem that at his best, Chaucer tries to help yet fails miserably as he relies on stereotypes, and at his worst, he tries to be negative but instead only highlights positive traits in women. However, though it would seem that he rests somewhere in the middle of the two conclusions, he does not. Without a doubt, Chaucer appears to write with a strong degree of negativity and misogyny, often pushing gender roles and strengthening the stereotypes women have sought to avoid and forget since their creation.

SOURCES

Baumgardner, Rachel. "I Alisoun, I Wife: Foucault's Three Egos and the *Wife of Bath's Prologue*." *Medieval Forum* (2006): 1-25. Retrieved 20 Nov. 2010.

Boro, Joyce. "John Fletcher's *Women Pleased* and the Pedagogy of Reading Romance." *Staging Early Modern Romance: Prose, Fiction, Dramatic Romance, and Shakespeare* (2009): 188-202. Retrieved 20 Nov. 2010.

Crawn, Edwin. "Allas, Allas! That Evere Love Was Synne: Excuses for Sin and the Wife of Bath's Stars." *The Hands of the Tongue* (2007): 33-60. Retrieved 6 Oct. 2010.

Driver, Martha. "Romancing the *Rose*: The Readings of Chaucer and Christine." *Writings on Love in the English Middle Ages* (2006): 147-162. Retrieved 20 Nov. 2010.

Harbus, Antonina. "Interpreting *The Wife of Bath's Prologue* and *Tale* in a Contemporary Note to Thynne's 1532 Edition." *Macquarie University* (2009): 3-11. Retrieved 20 Nov. 2010.

Hill-Vasquez, Heather. "Chaucer's Wife of Bath, Hoccleve's Arguing Women, and Lydgate's Hertord Wives: Lay Interpretation and the Figure of the Spinning Woman in Late Medieval England." *Florilegium* (2006): 169-195. Retrieved 6 Oct. 2010.

Normandin, Shawn. "The Wife of Bath's Urinary Imagination." *Exemplaria* (2008): 244-263. Retrieved 20 Nov. 2010.

O'Neill, Maria. "Gender, Economics and Morality: Sexuality and Ageing as Depicted in Geoffrey Chaucer's *The Canterbury Tales*." *Women Aging Through Literature and Experience* (2005): 73-82. Retrieved 20 Nov. 2010.

Partner, Nancy. "Studying Medieval Women: Sex, Gender, Feminism." *Speculum* (2010): 305-308. Retrieved 20 Nov. 2010.

Rasmussen, Mark David. "Feminist Chaucer? Some Implications for Teaching." *Studies in Medieval and Renaissance Teaching* (1997): 77-85. Retrieved 6 Oct. 2010.

Sadlek, Gregory. "Chaucer in the Dock: Literature, Women, and Medieval Antifeminism." *Studies in Medieval and Renaissance Teaching* (2007): 117-131. Retrieved 6 Oct. 2010.

Scala, Elizabeth. "Desire in the *Canterbury Tales*: Sovereignty and the Mastery Between the Wife and

Clerk." *Studies in the Age of Chaucer* (2009): 81-108. Retrieved 6 Oct. 2010.

Swinford, Dean. "Transforming the Trickster in Chaucer's *Wife of Bath's Tale.*" *Bloom's Literary Criticism* (2010): 229-238. Retrieved 6 Oct. 2010.

Tinkle, Theresa. "Contested Authority: Jerome and the Wife of Bath on I Timothy 2." *The Chaucer Review* (2010): 268-293. Retrieved 6 Oct. 2010.

Treharne, Elaine. "The Stereotype Confirmed? Chaucer's Wife of Bath." *Writing Gender and Genre in Medieval Literature: Approaches to Old and Middle English Texts* (2002): 93-114. Retrieved 20 Nov. 2010.

Walzem, Al. "Peynted by the Lion: The Wife of Bath as Feminist Pedagogue." *The Canterbury Tales Revisited* (2008): 44-59. Retrieved 6 Oct. 2010.

5. The Highs and Lows in the Treatment of Women

Man in Relation

The treatment of women is often a concern in works of literature. For this essay, the works of literature have varied greatly in terms of how women are treated. These works range from women being treated very badly, to greatly. For example, the Wife of Bath from Chaucer's *The Canterbury Tales* is treated poorly as she is not only verbally abused, but beaten as well. In addition, Spenser's wife from his wedding poem "Epithalamion" is treated very well as she is a figure of worship. Spenser loves her for her inner and outer beauty, and wants that message to be known for all time. Other females, such as Pertelote from Chaucer's *The Nun's Priest's Tale*, and the nun from *The Canterbury Tales*, fall somewhere in between these extremities. Of the relating works and texts, the Wife of Bath from Chaucer's *The Canterbury Tales* is treated the worst as she is subject to both physical and verbal harassment, and the unnamed wife from Spenser's "Epithalamion" is treated the best as she is wholeheartedly cherished.

The unnamed bride of Edmund Spenser is the best treated woman out of the works of literature read for this essay. Spenser's "Epithalamion" was a gift to his wife on their wedding day, and serves to praise his wife. The structure of the poem alone shows how much Spenser cares for his wife. In the poem, there are twenty four stanzas, and three hundred and sixty five long lines. These represent the hours in the day in the number of days in a year. The amount of effort put into the creation of the poem alone proves how well Spenser's wife was treated.

Spenser wants the reader to know how much he loves his wife. For example, at one point, he mentions that he is a faithful husband, and cares greatly for his wife (Spenser). Even though staying committed to his wife alone shows how much he loves her, he lists several other examples of how much he cares for his wife. One of the ways he shows his wife how much he cares is by praising her outer beauty. Spenser cares for her body so much that he does not want it to be too sunny on their wedding day, because she may become sunburned (Spenser). Additionally, Spenser describes his wife's body as being beautiful beyond measure. Physically, her body is unmatched, and Spenser wants the reader to know this fact.

Spenser continues in his description of his wife by explaining how her inner beauty is also unmatched. He knows that external beauty matters, but what truly matters is inner beauty (Spenser). Spenser feels as if the real her is what is inside, and cannot be seen. Inside and out, Spenser loves his wife, and it is difficult to find another woman who is treated so well.

Not only is his bride treated well on their wedding day, she is also praised for all time. Spenser wants both people and nature to celebrate their wedding day, and he wants it to be remembered forever (Spenser). Timelessness is a major theme within the poem, and it shows how great his love is for his wife. In fact, Spenser cherishes his wife to such an extent that he feels as if no other person has ever been as happy as they are (Spenser). His love for her is undying, and shows how well he treated her during his lifetime.

One of the better treated women in the works read for this essay is Madame Eglantine, from Chaucer's *The Canterbury Tales*. Most of her positive treatment comes from the people she encounters and the church as she is a nun. She is very extravagant for a nun, and is very well taken care of. She is dressed quite nicely, and has a good deal of expensive possessions. Some of those possessions would be small dogs which she takes with her (Chaucer). The nun even has enough extra money to feed her dogs better food than most people eat. With the money gained from both the people she encounters and her activities within the church, the nun is treated very well. Though her appearance is short, she ranks as one of the best treated women in any of the works read for this essay.

In Chaucer's *The Nun's Priest's Tale*, a female is treated badly.

Chanticleer's wife, Pertelote, is insulted and found to be untrustworthy. While Pertelote is not exactly a woman, she is a female figure with the human ability to talk. Therefore, though she might not literally be a human woman, she is still a female figure. Throughout the *Nun's Priest's Tale*, she is not treated the greatest by her male lover, Chanticleer. At one point, Chanticleer insults Pertelote in Latin, and this is damaging for two reasons. In addition to her being outright insulted by Chanticleer, her intelligence is insulted as well. This is due to the fact that she does not understand Latin, and Chanticleer knows this fact. However, when Chanticleer translates what he has just spoken to her, he makes it flattering and kind. Chanticleer fails in treating his primary lover well, and it is exposed through his insults.

As opposed to being insulted directly, Pertelote is also insulted indirectly. Chanticleer's poor treatment of his lover is further exposed when the reader learns of his many hens. It is explained by the Nun's Priest that Chanticleer has seven other hens to pleasure him (Chaucer). Strangely, some of the hens are even his sisters (Chaucer). Furthermore, the reader must question just how much the incestuous Chanticleer must care for Pertelote. She is only one of many different hens which serve one purpose: to sexually pleasure a single male. Pertelote is one of the more poorly treated women in the works read for this essay as she is insulted and disrespected both directly and indirectly.

Unsurprisingly, the Nun's Priest takes a break from telling his women-bashing story to bash more women. At one point during the storytelling, the Nun's Priest goes off on a tangent and decides to tell the group his opinion of women. He believes all women are troublemakers, and that they are all the sole cause of hardship (Chaucer). Additionally, he states that all women are evil, and that it all began with Eve. When the cowardly Nun's Priest realizes he is offending his boss, the nun, he ceases speaking about the subject (Chaucer). He then blames what he said to the group on Chanticleer, and claims the words he spoke are the rooster's. Realistically, the works spoken to the group were his, and he exposes himself as a patriarch. Women are

51

treated poorly both within and outside of the Nun's Priest's animal fable.

The Wife of Bath, from Chaucer's *The Canterbury Tales*, is treated poorly by both her husbands and Chaucer himself. She is treated poorly by Chaucer in the way he portrays women. He uses the Wife of Bath to make fun of women, and promote bad stereotypes. For example, the Wife of Bath enjoys talking quite a bit, and this goes along with the stereotype that women enjoy talking too much. The reader also discovers that she has cheated on her husbands (Chaucer). In addition, the reader later discovers that she accuses all of husbands of cheating on her (Chaucer). This is Chaucer's way of bashing the stereotype of women always being paranoid of their husbands cheating. Lastly, Chaucer makes her character nag quite a bit (Chaucer). None of these actions are helpful or beneficial to women, and only serve to damage their reputations.

The Wife of Bath is also treated poorly by her husbands. For example, one of her husbands used to enjoy reading to her about wicked wives in history (Chaucer). The book was originally meant for priests as a way of keeping them scared and weary of the evil of women. The priests who read this book often would understand that all women have ugly hearts, and are evil. This fact would keep them from straying from the church in order to find love and marriage. Therefore, the Wife of Bath's husband reading this book aloud to her is completely disrespectful as he is indirectly telling her that she is evil as well. The Wife of Bath was treated terribly as she was reminded of the supposedly evil wives of famous men in history. These men ranged from Sampson, who had his hair cut off by his wife, to Agamemnon, who was murdered after returning home from war. The book is entirely about the evils of women, and her husband reads it to her with the sole intention of reminding her of just how evil she is (Chaucer).

After some time, she is treated better by her husband, but it is not until after their relationship turns violent. When the Wife of Bath can no longer stand listening to her husband read aloud, she gets up and tears pages from his book. This angers him, and he strikes her with his fist

(Chaucer). With this act, the husband exceeds verbal harassment and commits an act of physical violence. None of the works read for this essay feature this sort of treatment of women. It is only after this physical violence that conditions improve and she is treated better. After this violent argument, she gains power in the relationship and they both happily get along. Moreover, it is because of this violence that the Wife of Bath is treated the worst out of all the other women in the works of literature examined for this essay.

The Wife of Bath and Spenser's unnamed wife are extreme opposites as one is treated poorly and the other is praised. Another poorly treated female aside from the Wife of Bath in Chaucer's *The Canterbury Tales* is Pertelote. Both of these females are constantly insulted, harassed and found to be untrustworthy. On the other hand, a few women were treated wonderfully in the works of literature read for this essay. The nun from Chaucer's *The Canterbury Tales* is doing financially well, and possesses a good deal of power. In addition, Spenser's unnamed bride experiences the best treatment as she is described as being an angelic and pristine woman. The works of literature read for this essay are diverse as they are host to all extremes, ranging from physical abuse and verbal harassment to compliments and timeless love.

SOURCES

Chaucer, Geoffrey. "General Prologue to The Canterbury Tales." Greenblatt 218-238.

Chaucer, Geoffrey. "The Nun's Priest's Tale." 298-312.

Chaucer, Geoffrey. "The Wife of Bath's Prologue and Tale." Greenblatt 256-284.

Greenblatt, Stephen, ed. *The Norton Anthology of English Literature*. New York: W. W. Norton & Company, Inc., 2006.

Spenser, Edmund. "Epithalamion." *The Norton Anthology of English Literature*. Ed. Stephen Greenblatt. New York: W. W. Norton & Company, Inc., 2006. 907-916.

6. A Full Circle Examination of Female Oppression in Bharati Mukherjee's *Jasmine*

Man as Stepping Stone

Performing a feminist reading often involves combing over a text and providing instances of oppression. However, when certain forms of oppression are made popular and others fall behind, the feminist reading falls short and is rendered incomplete. As a result, the partial feminist reading provides for a less strengthened argument, and the overall cause of the reading suffers. A solution for this issue is the "Power & Control Wheel" by Casa Myrna Vazquez, Inc. which provides for detailed summaries of the eight major forms of abuse. The chart helps to illuminate instances of less popular abuses such as isolation and financial control, while still helping to identify the more popular forms of oppression such as psychological and sexual abuse. The result of consulting Casa Myrna Vazquez's "Power & Control Wheel" is a thorough feminist reading of Bharati Mukherjee's *Jasmine* which locates and addresses the issue of oppression full circle.

Readers and critics alike tend to view the bildungsroman, or a coming-of-age novel, in a positive light, often noting the character's progress throughout the text. However, in Bharati Mukherjee's *Jasmine*, the road from start to finish is a grueling one marked with routine abuse. Lavina Dhingra Shankar's article "Activism, "Feminisms" and Americanization in Bharati Mukherjee's *Wife* and *Jasmine*" focuses on the positive elements of Jasmine's journey. She explains how the text is, "critically acclaimed as a positive affirmation of a poor, uneducated, Indian village girl's "metamorphosis, self-invention, and self-empowerment" (Chua, 57) in America" (Shankar 61). Her understanding of the novel is that it is about beneficial change taking place in several forms. On one hand, Jasmine experiences beneficial geographical change by escaping from an India plagued by conflict. She is liberated as she moves

54

further west, with her eventual goal being California. On the other hand, she experiences deep personal change as well. As the novel progresses, she is able to alter herself, commonly taking on new identities. Additionally, Shankar views her as strong given that her, "introduction to America is via a rapist, a Vietnam veteran, a man who perhaps symbolizes American imperialism in the "Third World"" (Shankar 65). With Jasmine overcoming the adversity and hardships throughout her travels, it would appear that there are few other ways to view her journey than positive. However, other critics disagree with this position. After reviewing the numerous instances of abuse and oppression in the novel, in all their forms, Mukherjee's *Jasmine* is instead cast in a negative light.

In order to better understand feminism and female oppression, it is important to note that abuse takes many shapes and forms. While certain abuses have been popularized, resulting in more media coverage, others remain out of sight. Unfortunately, as a result, they also drift far out of mind. In order to help solve this issue, Casa Myrna Vazquez, Inc. has developed the "Power & Control Wheel." Crafted by a Boston area organization bent on aiding women who are subject to abuse, the Power & Control Wheel is a chart meant to show and explain the eight major forms of abuse. The eight primary types of abuse are: psychological abuse, physical abuse, using privilege, financial abuse, verbal abuse, sexual abuse, intimidation, and isolation. Furthermore, understanding the dangers of each form of abuse is crucial in performing a feminist reading of the novel.

Psychological abuse is a major factor in *Jasmine*, even though it is not openly mentioned nearly as much as the other forms of abuse. Among other definitions, it explained by Casa Myrna Vazquez, Inc. as, "Playing mind games, exploiting immigration status, sexual orientation and/or disabilities. Also, minimizing concerns, ignoring feelings and placing blame" (CMV, Inc.). With that being said, it is expected that Jasmine is partly psychologically abused when she is raped by Half-Face in Florida. Not only is being raped a form of psychological abuse, but the murder that follows soon after is as well.

Her time in Florida, though brief when compared to other locations, hold a great deal of significance. Even the act of getting to Florida's shores is traumatic, and this is explained by Jasmine as she makes the journey. She explains, "I waded through Eden's waste: plastic bottles, floating oranges, boards, sodden boxes, white and green plastic sacks tied shut but picked open by birds and pulled apart by crabs" (Mukherjee 107). It appears as if traveling to Florida is a nightmare from start to finish, one sure to have lasting effects. Additionally, many other instances of psychological abuse occur throughout the novel. There are murders, rape, severe injuries, suicide, and even love affairs. One of the most significant events in the novel, playing its part to start Jasmine's journey, is the murder of her husband Prakash Vijh. The murder comes as Sukhwinder, a terrorist, detonates a bomb. This event alone is strong enough to set her on a quest to kill herself, an act regarded as nothing short of monumental. It is important to question what psychological effects there must have been in order to send a widow half way around the world, have her endure unbelievable amounts of pain, and finally end up committing suicide. Moreover, it is due to Prakash's death that the astrologer's prophecy, something heavily contested by Jasmine, is fulfilled. Lastly, as if Jasmine has not endured enough psychological abuse, her time in Iowa is one marked with confusion and hardship. The first incident renders her lover, Bud Ripplemeyer, paralyzed and stuck in a wheelchair. It occurs as a disgruntled Harlan Kroener takes his frustration out on Bud by shooting him. Witnessing the her lover being bound to a wheelchair is a powerful sight, and is topped only by Harlan then shooting himself. Though it would seem as if Iowa were a calm and quiet place, her time spent there is actually as defining as it is traumatizing.

Physical abuse does not occur frequently in *Jasmine*, but its several instances are shocking. It is defined as, "Hitting, choking, and/or burning. Threatening gestures. Forcing a victim to abuse alcohol and/or other drugs. Using weapons and/or other objects" (CMV, Inc.). Towards the beginning of the novel, physical abuse occurs as Jasmine is subject to a terrorist bombing that ends up killing her husband. She is not gravely injured, but what remains is the intent to kill. Moving onward, the primary event of physical abuse is when Jasmine is raped by Half-Face. Sami Ludwig's article titled "Cultural Identity as "Spouse,"" which focuses on limitations and possibilities in Mukherkee's *Jasmine*, explains the physical dangers of her journey. Ludwig clearly explains that "This middle passage is brutal" (Ludwig 106). With connotations to the era of African American slavery in the United States, the middle passage incites feelings of terror and fear. While Jasmine successfully makes the journey to Florida, the finish line is marked with disrespect and physical abuse. Moreover, when investigating the act of rape itself, it becomes clear that it is one of the most physically violent actions a person can perform next to murder. Raping another person involves potentially beating the victim, hurting them enough to make them submissive and fearful, followed by subduing them in order to prevent mobility. Even though the act of rape is a sexual one, it still involves much physical pain. This is true even during the sexual portion of the act itself. In fact, finding signs of forced entry is a trustworthy hint of a rape having commenced. With that being said, Jasmine endures a great deal of physical pain throughout the novel, even though it appears only occasionally as opposed to frequently.

The act of using privilege occurs quite often in *Jasmine*, allowing for Jasmine to be abused from the text's start to finish. It is defined as, "Always claiming to be right. Giving commands. Using religion, culture and/or gender-roles to impose authority" (CMV, Inc.). While there are subtle instances of her religion not being taken seriously, or her culture being more of a commodity, it is gender-roles that dominate this category. For example, the astrologer under the banyan tree in Hasnapur forecasts her future husband's death, her life as a widow, and even her fleeing the country. When she questions these claims, she is is disregarded as foolish, and is even hit on the head. It is a wound which leaves a noticeable scar. Despite the fact that this is only one man making predictions about Jasmine's future, his authority cannot be questioned. At the time, she is a young girl who is seen as more of a burden than anything else, and he is a figure trusted with predicting the futures of nearby residents.

Another instance of gender-roles coming into play comes as Jasmine wishes to remain in school. Traditionally, the young girls of Hasnapur would remain in school for approximately three years, and would then leave. With that statistic, it is only expected that she would not be taken seriously when she expresses her wish to remain in school. However, luckily for her, she is helped by both Masterji and her mother and eventually receives six years of schooling. The possible help of luck comes into play as it is nearly unbelievable to see her remain in school for such a long period of time. Even though it was something she felt strongly about, she was only a young girl at the time and had very little power or influence.

Yet another instance of gender-roles playing their part in *Jasmine* surfaces as Jasmine lives with Professorji. With him and the others, she is expected to follow the norms of a traditional Indian widow. Clearly, despite the fact that she does not wish to live this sort of life, her desires are disregarded. Suzanne Kehde sheds some light on the situation in her article "Colonial Discourse and Female Identity: Bharati Mukherjee's *Jasmine*." She explains that "Man is the focus of power. All the resources of the earth exist for his welfare and pleasure" (Kehde 71). In other words, it truly does not matter what Jasmine feels at this point, because she is not the focus. Professorji would rather live a traditional lifestyle, have her live the same lifestyle, and eat traditional Indian foods. Furthermore, given that women are ranked below men, Kehde feels as if, "This model provides the justification for the "natural" subordination of women to men..." (Kehde 71). While it may appear to be abuse to others, in Professorji's mind he is doing nothing out of the ordinary. Additionally, Carmen Wickramagamage helps to explain the situation a bit further in her article titled "The Empire Writes Back: Bharati Mukherjee's *Jasmine* as Post-Colonial Feminist Text." She explains how, "Social conventions consign the "unfortunate" widow to a form of desireless existence that is, in some ways, worse than death..." (Wickramagamage 65).

In other words, these social conventions act as a way of forcing women to be slaves to men. While this may seem odd to other cultures, it is important to remember this is a societal issue. To the traditional men of India, Jasmine being, "expected to occupy a subordinate position on account of her gender" is potentially seen as commonplace (Wickramagamage 76). These settings are unlike Iowa, where even her cooking is so radically different that she feels as if she is, "subverting the taste buds of Elsa County" (Banerjee 148). Unfortunately for Jasmine, the traditions of India seem to be very difficult from which to flee.

Financial abuse is a common event in *Jasmine*, with her often taking a subordinate position in relationships. It is defined as, "Controlling all decisions involving money. Interfering with choices involving work and education. Creating economic dependency" (CMV, Inc.). An instance of financial abuse surfaces early on in the novel when Prakash becomes angered over her having a job. She explains, "I panicked. For all his talk of us being equal, was he possessive about my working?" (Mukherjee 82). While Prakash certainly treats Jasmine kindly, even he subjects her to financial abuse. It is clear from the beginning that he controls their finances by determining where he will work and what he will do with his professional abilities. Jasmine states, "To want English was to want more than you had been given at birth, it was to want the world" (Mukherjee 68). With Prakash's ability to speak English, he received the better jobs and even determined that going to the United States was a financially beneficial idea as a result of receiving education. In other words, despite the positive imagery of them both being equal, he had control of their finances.

In order to grasp the financial abuse sustained by Jasmine, it is important to make note of her initial family. Jasmine was not born into extraordinary wealth, and was the fifth daughter out of a family of nine children. Growing up was challenging enough, but considering that she was fifth in line to be married adds a degree of difficulty. This sort of financial abuse appears to be livable on the surface, but there was the real potential that she would grow old and remain unmarried. While this is certainly fine in the United States, it is a real issue in *Jasmine*'s India as it is a male-dominated society. In addition, with her life in Hasnapur being difficult enough, her father was irresponsible with his money. It is noted that he wears extravagant clothing even though the family was quite poor. Lastly, Jasmine was so poor growing up that the quality of the United States was one of the first things she noticed. Upon using the shower after her rape, she believes it is, "a miracle, that even here in a place that looked deserted ... the tiles and porcelain should be clean, without smells, without bugs" (Mukherjee 117). Her earlier life was plagued by financial traditions such as dowries and hardship, resulting in her having little control or influence on financial decisions.

Verbal abuse is the first category to be mentioned that does not have a significant impact on the life of Jasmine. Aside from general disrespectful comments both intentional and unintentional, nothing stands out more than the language used by Half-Face. It is crucial to remember that he sees Jasmine as, "one prime little piece" (Mukherjee 115). Continuing with the vulgarity, he states "You know what's coming, and there ain't nobody here to help you, so my advice is lie back and enjoy it" before raping her (Mukherjee 115). As if the physical and psychological abuses were not enough, the verbal abuse witnessed in this scene demonstrates Half-Face's complete lack of respect for Jasmine. It is the most powerful instance of verbal abuse in the novel.

Sexual abuse is also infrequent, but its few instances are powerful. Casa Myrna Vazquez, Inc. defines it as, "Being forceful, threatening or coercive. Physically attacking body parts. Preventing the use of birth control and/or safe sex practices" (CMV, Inc.). While a few male characters, such as Darrel and Du, can be suggestive or hint at coerciveness, no single event compares to Jasmine's rape by Half-Face. In fact, he nearly defines the act of sexual abuse in full as he disregards Jasmine's feelings. He is forceful, because he has sex with her against her will. He is even coercive as he first speaks with her and attempts to reason his way into having sex with her. Also, he does attack her body parts as he forces her to have sex. In fact, Jasmine describes the act as being, "violent" (Mukherjee 116). Lastly, Half-Face even prevents the use of birth control and safe sex practices which can prevent the spread of sexually transmitted diseases and avoid pregnancy. Moreover, Jasmine even believes Half-Face to be, "from an underworld of evil" Mukherjee 116). No other sexual abuse in the novel comes close to this level of disrespect.

On a lighter note, other subtle instances of sexual abuse come while living in Iowa with Bud Ripplemeyer. While nothing compares to the sexual abuse witnessed in Florida, Jasmine does begin to suspect sexual tension is building between herself, Darrel and Du. The first instance occurs when Du witnesses Jasmine and Bud having sex in their bedroom. However, instead of removing himself from the situation, Du silently watches. Also, Darrel later confronts Jasmine about fleeing to New Mexico in order to make a new life for themselves. While these two events are worth mention, they do not compare to the horror in Florida experienced by Jasmine at the hands of Half-Face.

Intimidation is a subtle part of the text, but certainly contributes to the abuse found in the novel. Defined as, "Imposing fear by using looks and gestures. Destroying possessions. Threatening to call social service agencies and/or immigration authorities. Making threats involving children," there are a few events worth mention in *Jasmine*. The primary event is when Half-Face realizes he has the upper hand with Jasmine. He notices that Jasmine, "is so afraid of the Immigration and Naturalization Service that he can rape her with impunity, so docile he falls asleep while she is in the shower" (Kehde 71). Suzanne Kehde also states that Lillian Gordon, "scrutinizes Jasmine for marks of difference that must be erased lest they betray her to the Immigration and Naturalization Service..." (Kehde 71). Being a fearful illegal immigrant who has had two different people mention the Immigration and Naturalization Service to her, she is quick to get rid of her, "jeweled sandals," other personal effects, and even un-American traits such as finding escalators difficult to navigate (Kehde 71). Unfortunately for Jasmine, her past actions set her up to be intimidated by those similar to Half-Face. In "Always Becoming: Narratives of Nation and Self in Bharati Mukherjee's *Jasmine*," Deepika Bahri explains Jasmine's situation clearly. She writes that "Jasmine never becomes an American legally; in fact, she does not interact with "systemic" America at all. She remains undocumented, unmarked" (Bahri 141). Given Jasmine's immigration status, she is an easy target for intimidation.

Ending on a light note, isolation is arguably the easiest of the abuses to endure for Jasmine. It is defines as, "Limiting contact with friends and/or family. Restricting access to transportation. Monitoring phone calls" (CMV, Inc.). Despite the fact that Prakash appeared to be angry over Jasmine obtaining a job, she is not withheld from transportation. In fact, the entire novel can be defined as a frontier narrative, whose sole function is to tell the tale of a journey. While she does not take any friends or family from her home country and does the trip alone, nobody forces the isolation onto her. She makes the decision to venture westward to the United States, and even receives help doing it. When she finally arrives in the United States, she is taken in by several families and is almost never without company. Even though her company may be questionable at times, she is always in contact with others. Jasmine free to come and go as she pleases, and she does.

The "Power & Control Wheel" developed by Casa Myrna Vazquez, Inc. and used by numerous women's studies groups is invaluable in identifying and addressing instances of female oppression. It helps by providing the user with a chance to see the topic full circle with issues ranging from sexual abuse to intimidation, and physical abuse to isolation. With the help of the chart, it is possible to also locate verbal, financial and psychological abuses as well as the use of privilege. Bharati Mukherjee's *Jasmine* is full of abuse, with some being more prevalent than others. While there are subtle abuses faced by Jasmine such as being alone for a portion of her journey westward or being intimidated, there are abuses she faces that are nothing short of hellish. The absolute worst of the all, due to its psychological, sexual and physical effects to name a few, is the rape of Jasmine in Florida at the hands of Half-Face. Yet, these terrible events should never be ranked as each one helps to damage Jasmine. However, it is possible that some of the subtle abusive events could have either gone unnoticed or may not have been considered important if it were not for the "Power & Control Wheel." Considering the resulting clear and understandable picture, every aspect and element must be taken into account when female oppression is examined in full.

SOURCES

Bahri, Deepika. "Always Becoming: Narratives of Nation and Self in Bharati Mukherjee's *Jasmine*." *Women, America, and Movement: Narratives of Relocation*. Ed. Susan L. Roberson. Missouri: University of Missouri Press, 1998. 137-154. Print.

Banerjee, Mita. "The (Un)Translatability of Culture in Mukherjee's *Jasmine*." *Holding Their Own*. Eds. Dorothea Fischer-Hornung and Heike Raphael-Hernandez. Heidelberg, Germany: Stauffenburg, 2000. 143-152. *MLA Bibliography*. Web. 22 Nov. 2010.

Kehde, Suzanne. "Colonial Discourse and Female Identity: Bharati Mukherjee's *Jasmine*." *International Women's Writing: New Landscapes of Identity* (1995): 70-77. *MLA Bibliography*. Web. 22 Nov. 2010.

Ludwig, Sami. "Cultural Identity as "Spouse." *Fusion of Cultures* (1996): 103-110. *MLA Bibliography*. Web. 22 Nov. 2010.

Mukherjee, Bharati. *Jasmine*. New York: Grove Press, 1989. Print. *Power & Control Wheel*. 2007.

Casa Myrna Vazquez, Incorporated, Boston. *Casa Myrna Vazquez*. Web. 22 Nov. 2010.

Shankar, Lavina Dhingra. "Activism, "Feminisms" and Americanization in Bharati Mukherjee's *Wife and Jasmine*." *Hitting Critical Mass* 3.1 (1995): 61-84. *MLA Bibliography*. Web. 22 Nov. 2010.

Wickramagamage, Carmen. "The Empire Writes Back: Bharati Mukherjee's *Jasmine* as Post-Colonial Feminist Text." *Literary Studies East and West* (1996): 62-89. *MLA Bibliography*. Web. 22 Nov. 2010.

7. Similar Beginnings, Yet Differing Ends in *Sister Carrie* and *Maggie: A Girl of the Streets*

Man as Social Catalyst

Similar beginnings do not always result in similar ends. Examples of this are found in Dreiser's *Sister Carrie*, and Crane's *Maggie: A Girl of the Streets*. Both Carrie and Maggie begin their lives as part of the lower class and without much aid. However, after time, Carrie begins to rise steadily through the ranks of social standing, and Maggie falls considerably low. One reason for this is that Carrie seems to always date a man, grow bored of their life together, and move on. With Maggie, she is the one who is dumped. The result is two differing endings despite similar beginnings. Due to their relationships with men, both Carrie and Maggie share similar starts, yet experience different endings.

When Dreiser's *Sister Carrie* begins, Carrie is a very little fish who is headed to an incredibly large pond. At the moment she arrives in Chicago, she is without a job and ignorant of the world. As a result, she is vulnerable to all sorts of hardships and adversity. Adding to her potentially dangerous situation is the fact that Minnie is of little help to her, leaving her alone in an unforgiving city. When tallied, the odds are nothing short of against her. By the time she is settled in Chicago, her life is looking both grim and straining.

Within a short period of time, Carrie is able to improve her poor situation. Although she is an inexperienced woman with no history of work in an undoubtedly sexist time, she is able to find work. She finds work in a sweatshop, and, though the work is terrible, is provided with some spending money. Shortly after, she reestablishes a connection with Drouet, and is able to receive additional money and aid from him. For example, from the time they both sit down and eat at the restaurant, Drouet is disgusted by where she works. He explains, "You don't want to work at anything like that, anyhow" (Dreiser 43). As if his desire to help Carrie was not clear enough, he decides to hand her money. Forcing her to take the money, "...he slipped the greenbacks he had into her palm..." (Dreiser 45). The much-needed money and food signified not a simple act of kindness, but a new chapter in Carrie's life. From this point on, she would no longer be considered a part of the lowest tier of the lower class.

In Stephen Crane's *Maggie: A Girl of the Streets*, Maggie shares a similar beginning of her life with Carrie. Though the circumstances are not exactly equal, both women are from the lower class and are without enriched lives. Maggie grew up in a very poor neighborhood, plagued by violence and adversity. Near her house were the streets named Devil's Row and Rum Alley, and they were both as joyous as their names suggest. With such locations nearby, Maggie's house was almost fully enveloped in fighting factions, baseless and unmeasurable hatred, and poverty. Other than pure chance, there was not many ways to break free from this hostile environment.

Similar to Carrie's initial situation, Maggie's situation grows worse with time. Her brother, who once provided her with comfort, safety and love, grew to hate her immensely. David Fitelson supports this argument, mentioning how common it was that "...Jimmie wounds Maggie..." (Fitelson 187). Maggie's mother also grew more belligerent by the day. By the time Maggie had grown up and miraculously survived her childhood, she was used to being insulted, scolded and threatened by her closest family members.

With Drouet, Carrie was able to experience a new world. With so many improvements on nearly all aspects of life, Carrie quite literally ascended to a higher tier of living. Her clothes were finer, food was plentiful, meals were delicious, and entertainment became common. The new life she was living under Drouet's wings was revolutionary and thrilling. Though Carrie was definitely not close to being an upper class citizen, the contrast between the two lifestyles was astounding. However, her new life with Drouet would not remain exciting forever as it eventually grew stagnant. Within a short period of time, their relationship devolved considerably. For example, at one point he calls out to her by saying, "Where are you, Cad?" (Dreiser 74). The event shows his derogatory nature as he is, "...using a pet name he had given her." (Dreiser 74). This moment illustrates a turning point for Carrie, because the relationship has intolerably worsened. As Walter Michaels explains, "...Carrie has outgrown Drouet..." (Michaels 382). While she is certainly living a much better life than before meeting Drouet, it comes time for her to search for something better and more exciting.

Similar to Carrie, Maggie finds a way out of her situation and up the social ladder. Though her ascension is short-lived, the difference is refreshing. She meets Pete at a local saloon, and instantly becomes impressed by his higher standards of living. However, not all reactions to her decision to pursue Pete are positive. Her mother, "...could not conceive how it was possible for her daughter to fall so low as to bring disgrace upon her family" (Crane 168). Howard Horwitz explains how, "Maggie's family and neighbors routinely interpret her supposedly fallen conduct in biblical terms" (Horwitz 617). Everyone around her seems to understand her actions as borderline evil. Though, with the reality of her family hating her cast aside, Maggie fell deeply in love with Pete. Though he was only one step above her in social standing, it made a large difference. He could afford things she could not, and, as a result, she felt entertained when around him. For the first time in quite a while, she was happy and content with her life.

Seemingly arranged by fate, Carrie then meets Hurstwood and is provided with a perfect steppingstone to the upper class. In a coincidental manner, Hurstwood and Julia begin experiencing more extreme marital problems at the same point Carrie and Drouet are strained. Though the relationship appears to be fine on the surface, it is revealed that Hurstwood is displeased with its increasing staleness and repetition. It is explained that meals are, "...the kind that an ordinary servant can arrange" (Dreiser 63). Aside from the numerous other minor issues between them, such as problems with money and vanity, there was one incurable fact: there was no love left in the marriage (Dreiser 63). With that realization, both Hurstwood and Carrie were looking for ways out of their relationships. Carrie noticed Hurstwood to a minor extent, but it is Hurstwood who truly took interest in her. His desire for her, "...was the ancient attraction of the fresh for the stale" (Dreiser 75). To him, she was a way out, and a beautiful one at that. In addition, with the formation of their relationship, Carrie moved up to a higher class. Leaving Drouet behind, she rose to a slightly higher tier which featured more extravagance and entertainment.

Unlike Carrie, who becomes upset and bored with her current lover as often as the seasons change, Maggie continues loving Pete. However, her life changes altogether and she is left heartbroken when she discovers that Pete does not truly love her back. Joseph Brennan states how Pete has, "...driven Maggie away at last" (Brennan 305). She is shocked to see that he receives attention from and pays interest to high priced whores. When Pete leaves her in a drunken stupor, she is in disbelief and receives no support from the other women. Rather, they exclaim that she is a mere fool, and insult her. This event largely contrasts *Sister Carrie*, because it is the man who does the ditching. Also, as a result of being ditched, it is the woman who is left feeling hurt. In Ray West's essay, he mentions, "...natural impulses lead not to happiness, but to misfortune" (West 216). Unlike Carrie, her actions do not pay off.

After some time, it is Hurstwood who begins to greatly decline in social status. With a series of poor decisions, Hurstwood finds himself to be without his much loved job, wanted for arrest, and fleeing the city of Chicago. While Carrie does decide to stay with Hurstwood and weather the storm, she can only handle so much. Moreover, she decides to call it quits after Hurstwood moves to New York City, lands a mediocre job and is unable to afford many of the things he could before. Witnessing this decline first hand, Carrie decides to better both herself and the situation she is in. First, she vows to live an honest life and rise to a new tier in a moral sense (Dreiser 172). Then, she decides to rise above Hurstwood and his faltering mindset (Dreiser 199). After her much needed period of ascension, she comes to the realization that "True love she had never felt for him" (Dreiser 203). Carrie's realization initiates the beginning of the end for their relationship.

Though Carrie continuously progresses to a higher social standing throughout *Sister Carrie*, Maggie is caught in a downward fall. She is unable to escape these negative transitions, and sinks even lower after Pete is out of the picture. As Lawrence Oliver explains, "Maggie's unhappy world began to disintegrate..." (Oliver 656). Maggie's life consists of being hit on by other males, and, eventually, prostitution. For example, one drunken man says to her, "O'ny you left. Not half bad, though" (Crane 175). When left alone with this drunk, she is crudely admired and sought after. Furthermore, it is after this point in her life that she becomes enveloped in prostitution. Whereas Carrie improves herself to the point where she lands a successful acting career, Maggie is lost in the world of being a low cost whore. The result is a girl who is ultimately empty inside (Crane 183). Moreover, it seems as if any resemblance of the former, happy and youthful Maggie is effectively gone.

With a bit of luck and practice, Carrie finds her way to success. She has daydreams of past actresses she has witnessed, and these daydreams turn into desires. While sitting at home, doing nothing out of the ordinary, Carrie, "...remembered one beautiful actress – the sweetheart who had been wooed and won. The grace of this woman had won Carrie's heart" (Dreiser 220). From this point forward, acting is Carrie's primary concern. Delivering a wonderful performance could potentially send her to unimaginable heights and far away from Hurstwood's awful life. Luckily for her, her goals of becoming an actress are achieved, and she makes much more money than ever before. At this moment, "...Carrie's career progresses..." (Michaels 381). At last, she is able to leave Hurstwood and make a better life for herself. Additionally, she leaves the flat and gives Hurstwood "...twenty dollars" (Dreiser 307). With Hurstwood out of her way, she is able to achieve success and stardom. As the novel comes to a close, Carrie is a skillful and much appreciated actress who makes large sums of money. Furthermore, she finally rises to the upper class, completing a lengthy and unbelievably lucky transition. Rupin Desai states that "From this point on Carrie's success is assured" (Desai 309). Considering the fact that she began the transition as a poor and highly vulnerable girl, the outcome is outstanding. Hugh Witemeyer mentions her great transition, stating that "...the Carrie who has achieved fame in New York is not quite the same as the eighteen-year-old Carrie" (Witemeyer 314). It is clear that she has not simply changed, but changed for the better.

Though the specific event is debatable, Maggie ultimately dies an early death towards the end of the novel. Whether she saw how much her life had declined, and decided she was unable to live with herself, or a possible customer had turned violent, she dies at a young age. Though the death seems to be saddening, Maggie's mother is informed about the death in a cold manner. It is blatantly stated that "Mag's dead" (Crane 187). In addition, though they both began as part of the lower class, comparing this point in Maggie's life to Carrie and her stardom provides for great contrast. Carrie moved up through the ranks and saw her aspirations through with the help of luck, and Maggie moved up ever so slightly, only to fall completely. As a result, it is evident that Carrie rose to the highest social standing imaginable, while Maggie ceased to remain living.

Carrie and Maggie, due to their relationships with many men, head in opposite directions after sharing the same start. While they are both members of the lower class to begin with, their fates differ considerably. Carrie moves from being single, to dating increasingly higher class men, and then finally to leaving them both altogether. The end result is a woman whose life is nothing short of miraculous and lucky. On the other hand, Maggie grows attached to Pete, and it is he who ends up dumping her. Rather than being able to move up the social ladder, Maggie falls as the ending relationship destroys her. She ends up adopting a terrible lifestyle, and is eventually either murdered or commits suicide. Both Dreiser and Crane's stories, when juxtaposed, are perfect examples of how the beginning of a life does not determine where one will ultimately end up.

SOURCES

Brennan, Joseph. "Ironic and Symbolic Structure in Crane's Maggie." *Nineteenth-Century Fiction* 16.4 (1962): 303-315. *JSTOR*. Web. 21 Nov. 2009.

Crane, Stephen. "Maggie: A Girl of the Streets." *Great Short Works of Stephen Crane*. New York: Perennial, 2004. 127-189.

Desai, Rupin. "Delusion and Reality in Sister Carrie." *PMLA* 87.2 (1972): 309-310. *JSTOR*. Web. 21 Nov. 2009.

Dreiser, Theodore. *Sister Carrie*. Ed. Donald Pizer. New York: W. W. Norton & Company, 2006. 1-355.

Fitelson, David. "Stephen Crane's "Maggie" and Darwinism." *American Quarterly* 16.2 (1964): 182-194. *JSTOR*. Web. 21 Nov. 2009.

Horwitz, Howard. "Maggie and the Sociological Paradigm." *American Literary History* 10.4 (1998): 606-638. *JSTOR*. Web. 21 Nov. 2009.

Michaels, Walter. ""Sister Carrie"'s Popular Economy." *Critical Inquiry* 7.2 (1980): 373-390. *JSTOR*. Web. 21 Nov. 2009.

Oliver, Lawrence. "Brander Matthews' Re-visioning of Crane's Maggie." *American Literature* 60.4 (1988): 654-658. *JSTOR*. Web. 21 Nov. 2009.

West, Ray. "Stephen Crane: Author in Transition." *American Literature* 34.2 (1962): 215-228. *JSTOR*. Web. 21 Nov. 2009.

Witemeyer, Hugh. "Sister Carrie: Plus ca Change." *PMLA* 87.3 (1972): 514. *JSTOR*. Web. 21 Nov. 2009.

8. Postmodern Memory in Toni Morrison's *Beloved* and Christopher Nolan's *Memento*

Man as Historical Architect

Memory can be found in countless stories both new and old. However, within recent decades it has been subjected to a postmodern twist. Specifically examining the roles of memory in Toni Morrison's *Beloved* and Christopher Nolan's *Memento*, the two texts present differing takes on memory. In *Beloved*, the main character Sethe can no longer flee from her past as physical objects and areas begin causing flashbacks. However, in *Memento*, the role of memory is arguably more important. The main character Leonard is able to shape his present and direct his future as he manipulates his own memories. Furthermore, memory appears in both texts in a variety of ways. In *Memento*, the only way Leonard can recall his short-term memories is to make keepsakes such as photographs, notes, and even permanent tattoos. And in *Beloved*, memory serves to remind Sethe that she cannot avoid her past forever. She experiences flashbacks at certain locations by viewing various objects that mind her of her traumatic past. Toni Morrison's *Beloved* and Christopher Nolan's *Memento* demonstrate how differing texts, crafted years apart and set centuries apart, relate by presenting two uniquely postmodern takes on memory.

The topics of memory and rememory are crucial in Toni Morrison's *Beloved* and Christopher Nolan's *Memento*. Defined as events that are recorded and available for remembering at a later date, memory appears often in *Memento*. Jo Alyson Parker, author of "Remembering the Future: *Memento*, the Reverse of Time's Arrow, and the Defects of Memory," explains Leonard's predicament in stating he, "can no longer engage in the process of consolidation whereby short-term memories are converted into long-term ones" (Parker 240). In other words, his ability to remember short-term memories is compromised, resulting in a strange method of constructing memory. However, in *Beloved,* the main character Sethe experiences rememory, or the act of unconsciously, unintentionally bumping into memories. Whereas rememory is unconsciously done, memory is done consciously. In Michael Trussler's "Spectral Witnesses: The Doubled Voice in Martin Amis's *Time's Arrow*, Toni Morrison's *Beloved* and Wim Wenders' *Wings of Desire*," he states that "angels and other spectral onlookers provide what Toni Morrison calls a "rememory" or events, an uncanny encounter with temporality" (Trussler 29). Meaning, given the nature of time and its ability to be fluid in the postmodern, events are able to be pulled out of the past and remembered. Toni Morrison's novel features this "phenomenon" often, helping to suggest, "the immeasurability of the present" (Trussler 29). The two concepts similarly deal with the function of the past and its remembrance, with the difference being whether or not the act of remembering is an unconscious or conscious one.

Examining the key ideas behind memory and rememory is crucial in understanding what it means to consciously or unconsciously perform an action. In *Beloved*, the act of remembering is usually unconsciously triggered for Sethe. For example, specific areas and objects within her surrounding environment may bring memories of the dreaded Sweet Home to mind. As for *Memento*, memory is wholly different. With Leonard's long-term memories still intact, it is specifically his short-term memory that is damaged and requires reminders. Also, with his memories being constructed, it is assumed that Leonard's form of remembering takes a degree of intelligence. He must sift through the vast amounts of information that is not true in order to find truth, or what he believes is truth. Furthermore, while Sethe relies on the temporal, Leonard relies on the spatial. The objects occupying his spatial realm are keepsakes, better known as mementos, the very nature of the film's title. These memory-aiding mementos are an element of postmodernity, because they keep him on the surface by not allowing him to dig deeper. In other words, when solely addressing his short-term memory, he is only able to comprehend minimal amounts of information. Leonard's memories are organized and interpreted in a completely opposite manner from Sethe's memories.

Another key difference between memory in *Beloved* and *Memento* is construction. In *Beloved*, Sethe is arguably capable of reinterpreting her past differently than everyone else, but is unable to reconstruct her past similar to Leonard. An example of Leonard constructing his past comes as he burns certain images to eliminate grief, and to selectively remember. He demonstrates that memories can be created in the present and are sometimes determined by needs in the present. Even though his ability to construct memories makes him an unreliable narrator, his actions are crucial in showing viewers how constructed memories turn to facts. Pursuing this topic further is Diran Lyons in his article "Vengeance, the Powers of the False, and the Time-Image in Christopher Nolan's *Memento*." He begins by explaining that "memory, if not reduced to mere chemical processes in the brain, is both past and present simultaneously" (Lyons 128). This fact is due to Leonard's ability to shape and mold his memories in the present. In doing so, he is able to, "present temporality and a living past within memory" (Lyons 128). In other words, with his crafting comes not a static past, but instead one that lives and breathes. Continuing, Lyons notes how Leonard makes a conscious effort to construct, "objects of memory" (Lyons 128). Without these objects, his already ineffective short-term memory would be rendered even worse. Lastly, though there are differences between Sethe and Leonard's methods for remembering the past, they are not unalike. Both main characters are mentally damaged due to past events. For Sethe, it is her traumatizing past as a slave and a runaway, and for Leonard it is the death of his wife following a supposed break in. To better grasp the similarities and differences of Leonard and Sethe, it is important to investigate their stories in search of instances where memory has been the focus.

Toni Morrison's *Beloved* provides both a differently functioning memory as well as instances of rememory. By definition, most instances of

73

rememory occur as Sethe unintentionally bumps into her memories. For example, Beloved herself functions in this way, reminding Sethe of her gruesome past. Another instance would be whenever Sethe ventures to the Clearing. Part way through the novel, Sethe arrives at the Clearing and sees Baby Sugg's, "old preaching rock" and instantly begins remembering the past (Morrison 111). She remembers, "the smell of leaves shimmering in the sun, thunderous feet and the shouts that ripped pods off the limbs of the chestnuts" (Morrison 111). Progressively getting worse, Sethe's memories turn from tranquil to destructive. However, after initially recollecting the past, she remembers simpler times consisting of other, "[negro] views, habits; where they had been and what done; of feeling their fun and sorrow along with her own" (Morrison 111). While her memories are not as negative as they could be at this point, they still explain her sorrow. Despite her sorrowful account, she explains that moving away from the area meant moving, "away from the enchantment of the Clearing" (Morrison 115). This instance of rememory is timid in comparison to events that would come later.

Soon after the experiences at the site of the Clearing, Sethe has flashbacks to her interactions with schoolteacher. She explains that "her spirits fell down under the weight of the things she remembered and those she did not: schoolteacher writing in ink she herself had made" (Morrison 116). Still triggering rememory due to her time at the Clearing, she is unable to focus on the present. In her article titled "Embodiment of Trauma: Corporeality in Toni Morrison's *Beloved*," Hanna Reinikainen explains this portion of Sethe's past. She writes, "the character of Schoolteacher makes his pupils do an exercise of writing the farm's slaves' human and animal characteristics on different sides of their papers" (Reinikainen 96). According to her, this is to show the differences between whites and blacks. She then points out how many believed there were fundamental differences between whites and blacks in both body and mind. She states, "in the black body, the mind is reduced to a minimum," while it is the opposite case for whites (Reinikainen 97). If racist theories are believed, Sethe is unable to clearly remember her past due to her biological limitations. With that being said, Reinikainen then touches on the issue of the baby ghost, and its possible meaning.

Hanna Reinikainen and Paul Neubauer both address the presence of the baby ghost in the novel. Given her research, Reinikainen believes its function is clearly explained by examining tradition. She writes, "Why has Morrison used a ghost? Kathleen Brogan has said that ghosts in ethnic and women's literature function as "outlaw versions of their former social invisibility" (Brogan 25)" (Reinikainen 99). Again, an object triggers Sethe to recount the former, or the past. Reinikainen continues, "Beloved thus functions as a kind of condensed embodiment of all the untold stories of the victims of slavery" (Reinikainen 99). Not purely functioning on behalf of Sethe, Beloved forces other African Americans to examine their pasts in the same way that other objects have worked exclusively for Sethe. Beloved is an object of remembrance. Continuing where Reinikainen left off with his article "The Demons of Loss and Longing: The Function of the Ghost in Toni Morrison's *Beloved*," Paul Neubauer attempts to show how Beloved is memory you cannot run from. Unlike other memory-triggering objects in Sethe's environment, Beloved is different. Neubauer explains how, "Beloved came out of the water, the traditional boundary between the domain of the living and the land of the dead" (Neubauer 167). Even from beyond the grave, Beloved appears and forces Sethe to remember her past. Of the many physical items that conjure up painful memories, the baby ghost is the most efficient as Sethe cannot prepare for her, nor can she be avoided.

Beloved herself functions as a breathing, walking reminder of the past from which Sethe cannot hide. Exploring the role of Beloved in the novel is Emily Jeremiah with her article "Murderous Mothers: Adrienne Rich's *Of Woman Born* and Toni Morrison's *Beloved*." Jeremiah entertains the idea of having a positive view of Sethe's past, stating that she, "murders her baby girl out of desperate love, wanting to keep her safe from the horror of slavery" (Jeremiah 63). This idea holds truth as there are no upsides to Sethe's experience as a slave. Jeremiah mentions, "The "tree" of scars on Sethe's back, from the whipping inflicted upon her when she was pregnant" (Jeremiah 64). It is a, "visible imprint of slavery," and continues the theme of memories in the past determining feelings in the future (Jeremiah 64). With these painful memories in mind, Sethe decides to murder her child out of protection. Moreover, little amounts of anything are needed from the physical realm in order to remind her of her past. In this case, she is being pursued by schoolteacher, and is in a state of continuous rememory. In addition, the memories Sethe experiences are subject to interpretation. For members of her neighborhood, they are, "the community's shared memories" that they all must deal with (Jeremiah 67). On the other hand, not everyone who remembers Sethe's past is African American. Jeremiah explains how, with it being seen from the perspective of schoolteacher, "that insanity, that despair, is subject to white interpretation" (Jeremiah 65). In other words, while Jeremiah believes Sethe's actions to be out of love, others may view it plainly as the, "murder [of] her daughter" (Jeremiah 66). Whatever the interpretation, the sad fact remains that Sethe ended her daughter's life in an attempt to save her from slavery, and it is an act that which comes back to literally haunt her later in life.

With a past as haunting as the one witnessed in *Beloved*, it is nearly expected that even subtle events can serve as reminders. An instance of rememory on Paul D's behalf comes after viewing Beloved. The narrator explains his past, "Move. Walk. Run. Hide. Steal and move on. Only once had it been possible for him to stay in one spot" (Morrison 78). Paul D's past is riddled with instances of hunger, extreme survival and even hiding in caves. Many of these traumatic events have been tucked away in his tobacco tin, a safe location for memories too painful to continuously remember. Furthermore, Sethe also suffers due to events that subtly trigger rememory. When all three women are sharing a narrative in a blended stream of consciousness, it is spoken out that "Sethe is the one that picked flowers, yellow flowers in their place before the crouching. Took them away from their

76

green leaves" (Morrison 253). This statement which is seemingly based on flowers alone could be implying that Sethe hurt Beloved while she was still green, or still young. With both Paul D and Sethe having their pasts resurface, it seems as if nearly everything has the potential to trigger rememory.

Stamp Paid is another person to witness past memories resurface. When Sethe and others within the house at 124 are experiencing a powerful episode of seemingly paranormal activity triggered by rememory, Stamp Paid is able to witness the event. The narrator explains how, "although he couldn't cipher but one word, he believed he knew who spoke them" (Morrison 253). The narrator then plainly states, "what a roaring" (Morrison 253). Hinting that the paranormal episodes in the house deal with the past, Stamp Paid finds himself believing the activity was, "the mumbling of the black and angry dead" (Morrison 234). The past and its memories surface within the chapter, becoming real and physical entities that even others outside of the immediate family can witness.

Similar to Sethe, in Christopher Nolan's *Memento* the main character also has odd experiences with memory. In the movie, it functions differently as Leonard constructs his past and reshapes his memories. Typically, he leaves himself mementos in order to remind himself of something at a later date, long after his short-term memory has reset itself. These items could be tattoos, notes or even photographs. With these items, he reconstructs his past piece by piece, allowing himself to experience a present that is fluid and changing.

Beginning with his memory in general, Leonard has an odd way of keeping track of memories by making a conscious effort to stay organized. He explains, "You know, I can remember so much. The feel of the world... her. [*sighs*] She's gone. And the present is trivia, which I scribble down as fucking notes" (*Memento*). As Leonard mentions, he is unable to rely on his short-term memories becoming long-term memories, so he is forced to scribble down whatever he can in order to remember his recent past.

77

Additionally, Leonard has a functioning long-term memory which requires no constructing. He explains his take on long-term memory to the viewer, painting an unhappy scene. Leonard states, "There are things you know for sure. I know what that's going to sound like when I knock on it. I know what that's going to feel like when I pick it up. See? Certainties. It's the kind of memory that you take for granted" (*Memento*). Unfortunately for Leonard, he learns the hard way how to appreciate his long-term memory after dealing with a practically nonexistent short-term memory. As a result, his present is a miserably confusing place where nothing is solid or set, but is instead fluid, leaving him to pursue his wife's killer in an odd manner.

Whatever the actual cause, the death of Leonard's wife is his motivation throughout the movie. A scene with a friendly bartender sheds some light on the situation, "Natalie: What's the last thing you remember? Leonard: My wife... Natalie: That's sweet. Leonard: ...dying" (*Memento*). It is his explanation in this event that drives him and gives his life meaning. However, though it gives Leonard's life purpose it is still saddening. Whether or not the sorrow felt by Leonard is feigned as a result of psychological instability, the event itself gives him memories to recall in order to stay motivated.

Through all of the time Leonard has stayed driven to find his wife's killer, he has been reconstructing his recent past. Explaining the power of memory, Leonard states that "Memory can change the shape of a room; it can change the color of a car. And memories can be distorted. They're just an interpretation, they're not a record, and they're irrelevant if you have the facts" (*Memento*). In other words, he is explaining exactly what he does on a daily basis. He rewrites history and creates his own facts, refusing to believe that memory is solid. Furthermore, when something needs to change, he changes it by literally rewriting history. As a result, the present is fluid and alterable. In addition, in a telling scene where crooked cop Teddy converses with Leonard, truth is exposed. Teddy speaks to Leonard, saying, "You don't know who you are anymore. Leonard: Of course I do. I'm Leonard Shelby. I'm from San Francisco" (*Memento*). With that being said, it appears as if Leonard may have a grip on his past and may be on the right course. However, Teddy then corrects him, saying, "No, that's who you were. Maybe it's time you started investigating yourself" (*Memento*) Within an instant, Leonard's routine is exposed and it appears as if he has been reconstructing his memories in order to transform himself. George Bragues' article "Memory and Morals in *Memento*" explains Leonard's current discovery, stating, "his memory problem hampers his ability to sustain lengthy undertakings" (Bragues 62). Leonard is unable to efficiently commit to anything lengthy as he rewrites what he was doing, transforms and eventually changes course altogether. Teddy has witnessed this, and has made note of Leonard's transformation since San Francisco. Bragues explains how, "Teddy insists that Leonard has since reconstructed his memory of the events to veil a terrible truth about his past and lend purpose to his existence" (Bragues 62-63). Similar to Sethe, his past contains painful events that are too terrible to accurately recall. His solution is to cover up said events so that he may move onward, even if it may be in the wrong direction.

The story of Sammy Jankis within the narrative reveals information about Leonard and his interactions with memory. Leonard explains, "Sammy Jankis wrote himself endless notes. But he'd get mixed up. I've got a more graceful solution to the memory problem. I'm disciplined and organized. I used habit and routine to make my life possible" (*Memento*). However, even with his system of keepsakes ranging from tattoos to photos, it is questionable just how organized his memories really are. In a way, his constant reminders to, "remember Sammy Jankis" and tell his story actually begin to show their similarities, not their differences (*Memento*). Venturing back to Jo Alyson Parker's article titled "Remembering the Future: *Memento*, the Reverse of Time's Arrow, and the Defects of Memory," she makes note of the situation in stating, "Sammy, too, had anterograde amnesia" (Parker 244). She then explains, "Leonard rehearses the story of Sammy's inability to condition himself as a means of reminding himself to do so" (Parker 244).

This fact points out how Leonard is not much better off than Sammy Jankis himself as he is not fully organized with his memories. While continuing to point out their similarities, Parker ponders about a possible reality. She writes, "Sammy Jankis's diabetic wife manipulated Sammy into killing her. In fact, Sammy's story may actually be Leonard's projection of his own situation onto Sammy." (Parker 248). Whether or not they are the same person, both are similar in that they have difficult memory problems as well as an inability to stay fully organized with their memories.

While Leonard may appear to rest somewhere in between the two emotions, Leonard's memory condition is depressing as opposed to motivating. Late in the film, he does express his satisfaction with his life having meaning given its current layout. He is able to be in constant pursuit of his goals, and is always able to consciously alter his memories if need be. However, his long-term memory is depressing. "Surviving *Memento*," by William Little, reminds viewers that Leonard's life was turned upside down, and that he lives in constant pain due to his memories. On the brighter side, one example of *Memento*'s comical nature is Leonard's repeating of the line, "I have this condition" (*Memento*). However, while select elements are comical, Little explains that there is pain involved and that it is revealed with, "one tattoo [proclaiming] "Memory is treachery"" (Little 73). Little then explains how, "The memory prompted by the memento is not quite one of domestic bliss" (Little 75). Both Leonard and Little are aware of the sorrow involved in memory. As for Leonard, he speaks about his actions regretfully, stating, "I'm not a killer. I'm just someone who wanted to make things right" (*Memento*). Whatever Leonard's true intentions or psychological status, he is unable to feign being happy as he shows the audience many signs that he is not.

While both stories consist of main characters who are pained by their memories, the memory found in *Beloved* and *Memento* have different functions. In *Beloved*, Toni Morrison relies on a straightforward method of traditional storytelling. Sethe's memories force her to face the past she once

80

ignored, engaging in rememory. Moreover, Sethe has the postmodern ability to view an object and experience hallucination-like flashbacks. With her present being plagued by vivid trips into the past, she is stuck remembering painful memories she seeks to forget. On the other hand, Christopher Nolan's *Memento* features a more radical method of recounting the past. Leonard is able to construct his past in the present, and does so by telling the story of his short-term memories backwards. Verena-Susanna Nungesser touches on this topic in "I Forgot to Remember (to Forget)," writing, "By constantly making up his own truth *Memento*'s protagonist reminds us of the creative and "constructive nature of autobiographical remembering"" (Nungesser 39). Unlike Sethe who only experiences flashbacks and is unable to reconstruct, Leonard is able to form, "his narrative identity, by constructing the kind of dynamic identity found in the plot" (Nungesser 39). In addition, *Beloved* and *Memento* differ in terms of structure. Toni Morrison sticks to a linear storyline that only briefly recalls the past. However, Nolan's *Memento* is a mixture of forward and backward storytelling. This postmodern method of structuring the narrative is complex yet understandable as short-term memories venture backwards and long-term memories move forwards. Despite the few similarities they share, *Beloved* and *Memento* are different in both structure and memory.

Christopher Nolan's *Memento* and Toni Morrison's *Beloved* are structured around postmodern ideas of memory. In *Memento*, memory functions as a fluid part of Leonard's past. If there are elements of his short-term memory which cause pain, he can overwrite them to the point where even he begins to take on a new identity. As for *Beloved*, memory functions as a way of forcibly remembering the past. Numerous instances of memory appear in *Memento*, ranging from Teddy revealing parts of Leonard's past to Leonard reading off the tattoos on his body. In *Beloved*, memory surfaces whenever she witnesses something that reminds her of her slave past, such as a certain rock or even hair. Also, whereas Leonard makes a conscious effort to rewrite his memories, Sethe unintentionally bumps into her past after being triggered by physical objects. While *Memento* and *Beloved* relate in allowing memory to have an important role, its use in both texts remains uniquely postmodern.

SOURCES

Bragues, George. "Memory and Morals in *Memento*." *Film-Philosophy* 12.2 (2008): 62-82. *MLA Bibliography*. Web. 22 Nov. 2010.

Brogan, Kathleen. *Cultural Haunting: Ghosts and Ethnicity in Recent American Literature*. Charlottesville: UP of Virginia, 1998. Web.

Eakin, Paul John. *How Our Lives Become Stories: Making Selves*. Ithaca: Cornell UP, 1999. Web. International Movie Database, The. "Memento." *The International Movie Database, Ltd.* Web. 10 Dec. 2010.

Jeremiah, Emily. "Murderous Mothers: Adrienne Rich's *Of Woman Born* and Toni Morrison's *Beloved*." *From Motherhood to Mothering* (2004): 59-71. *MLA Bibliography*. Web. 22 Nov. 2010.

Little, William. "Surviving *Memento*." *Narrative* 13.1 (2005): 67-83. *MLA Bibliography*. Web. 22 Nov. 2010.

Lyons, Diran. "Vengeance, the Powers of the False, and the Time-Image in Christopher Nolan's *Memento*." *Journal of the Theoretical Humanities* 2.1 (2006): 127-135. *MLA Bibliography*. Web. 22 Nov. 2010.

Memento. Dir. Christopher Nolan. Perf. Guy Pearce, Carrie-Anne Moss, and Joe Pantoliano. New Market, 2001. Film.

Morrison, Toni. *Beloved*. New York: Vintage International, 1987. Print.

Neubauer, Paul. "The Demon of Loss and Longing: The Function of the Ghost in Toni Morrison's *Beloved*." *Demons; Mediators Between This World and the Other; Essays on Demonic Being From the Middle Ages to the Present* (1998): 165-174. *MLA Bibliography*. Web. 22 Nov. 2010.

Nungesser, Verena-Susanna. "I Forgot to Remember (to Forget): Personal Memories in *Memento* (2000) and *Eternal Sunshine of the Spotless Mind* (2004)." *Mediation, Remediation, and the Dynamics of Cultural Memory* (2009): 31-47. *MLA Bibliography*. Web. 22 Nov. 2010.

Parker, Jo Alyson. "Remembering the Future: *Memento*, the Reverse of Time's Arrow, and the Defects of Memory." *KronoScope* 4.2 (2004): 239-257. *MLA Bibliography*. Web. 22 Nov. 2010.

Reinikainen, Hanna. "Embodiment of Trauma: Corporeality in Toni Morrison's *Beloved*." *Close Encounters of an Other Kind: New Perspectives on Race, Ethnicity and American Studies* (2005): 95-102. *MLA Bibliography*. Web. 22 Nov. 2010.

Ricoeur, Paul. "Life in Quest of Narrative." Transl. David Wood. New York: Routledge, 1991. Web.

Trussler, Michael. "Spectral Witnesses: The Doubled Voice in Martin Amis's *Time's Arrow*, Toni Morrison's *Beloved* and Wim Wenders' *Wings of Desire*." *Journal of the Fantastic in the Arts* 14.1 (2002): 28-50. *MLA Bibliography*. Web. 22 Nov. 2010.

9. A Historical Look at Jane Austen's *Sense and Sensibility*

The Feeling of Man

Since the term was created, sensibility has drastically changed literature, forever holding a place in history. Examining the history of the concept provides for many interesting discoveries, such as the fact that the term first arrived long before it was included in any novel. Though, within a few centuries, sensibility would be the primary focus of novels. Its chance to take the spotlight would come after the world began focusing on science, and its ability to render what was once misunderstood explainable. While many people turned to formulas, calculations and numbers, others insisted on the idea that not all elements in life were so easily explained. For example, though felt, experienced and witnessed, emotions were not able to be put into numbers. Emotions and sensations stemmed from the experiencing of events, and this concept is the basis of the novel of sensibility. The ability to feel was tested by novels of sensibility, and some were exceptional. Samuel Richardson's *Clarissa* consisted of an angelic young heroine being mercilessly tortured for a great deal of time, and Henry Mackenzie's *The Man of Feeling* provided readers with an emotional man. Though these two novels were masterly in their own right, Jane Austen's *Sense and Sensibility* would revolutionize the genre. *Sense & Sensibility*, by Jane Austen, revolutionizes the novel of sensibility as it hosts extreme emotion.

The concept of sensibility first arrived in the 15th century, and is paired with a number of definitions. To some, it is known as the, "ability to receive sensations," or a, "refined or excessive sensitiveness in emotion and taste with especial responsiveness to the pathetic" (Merriam-Webster). The former definition applies to the reader, as novels of sensibility often contain moments of extreme sensation. However, the latter definition applies to novels of sensibility, and their extreme focus on pathetic characters who are often tortured in a variety of ways. The chance to experience extreme sensation was one benefit to reading novels, and, as a result, the novel soon flourished. The arguable height of sensibility in novels, defined by readers' overwhelming amount of interest, came when Jane Austen, Samuel Richardson and Henry Mackenzie released *Sense & Sensibility, Clarissa,* and *The Man of Feeling* respectively. Furthermore, though novels written today certainly conjure up emotions and sensations within readers, the novel of sensibility soon declined in popularity. Novelists would soon take on other endeavors, as opposed to focusing their writing on one weighty, unbelievable, and overly tortured character. However, with that being said, it is important to note that sensibility is still a large part of our culture as many seek to feel strong emotions as a result of experience.

Centuries after the appearance of the word, sensibility made its way into English literature. Also, novels rose greatly in popularity as they provided readers with lengthy and emotion provoking ordeals. The ability to receive sensations became important, not only because they tend to shape the overall tone and feeling of the novel, but because they tested the reader. In reading a gripping and generally saddening novel, readers' ability to feel through experience was tested. Furthermore, it is important to note that being able to feel served many functions. In a minimal sense, reading novels of sensibility fine tuned your ability to deal with saddening events in life. To a certain extent, reading about angelic protagonists being emotionally and psychologically tortured desensitized the reader. Also, the ability to feel sensations defined whether or not the reader was human and had a heart. If some ghastly action were to occur in the novel, it meant a lot if the reader could feel emotion from experiencing it. If the reader is unable to, the lack of emotion indirectly says quite a bit about them. Lastly, the recreational reading of novels of sensibility was a mark of sophistication. To be able to read such novels and casually feel the gripping pain they provide was a admirable trait. Though the novel of sensibility was somewhat short-lived, their influence and presence is still felt today.

The Age of Sensibility came during an interesting time in English literature. Developing alongside the age was the Age of Reason. The Age of Reason was entirely science-based, and put large amounts of meaning into numbers and formulas. Many argued that the supposedly enlightening age rendered life colder and less personal. The Age of Reason, though beneficial in countless ways varying from medicine to machinery, was thought to have taken the magic out of life. As a result, much of the unknown world was soon explainable or soon on its way to being understood, even if partially. However, the Age of Sensibility went against such notions and ideas. It promoted the idea that certain elements of life were not so easily understood. To those in opposition to the Age of Reason, not everything could be measured, calculated, or put into formulas. Emotion and sensation were two such elements of life which were believed to be nearly unexplainable. For one, emotion was equally as complex as science, yet not so easily defined. Moreover, much in the world of emotion remained confusing, and science failed to apply its impersonal and disenchanting explanations to it. Through the reading of novels of sensibility, people could experience what science could not explain.

Following the Age of Sensibility was the short-lived Age of Romanticism. The ages relate to each other as they were both near opposites of the Age of Reason. When science gained speed and significantly improved technology, many began believing in the tenets of the Age of Romanticism. As opposed to being cold and calculated, romantics returned to nature and emotion. Additionally, while it is true that romantic literature's primary focus was the loss of nature, there were similarities to novels of sensibility. For example, The Scarlet Letter could easily be viewed as a novel of sensibility with less intensity. The entire novel focuses on the suffering, and emotional torture of a woman who has simply made a mistake early on in life. Samuel Richardson's Clarissa does the same, just to a much fuller extent. In conclusion, though the Age of Sensibility and the Age of Romanticism have their differences, both fought science's attempt to explain everything in life. There was much more to life than cold calculations, formulas and technology.

Samuel Richardson's *Clarissa* was published in 1748, and provided readers with the gripping tale of a young woman being tortured physically, emotionally, and psychologically. As a whole, the novel was well received as readers were able to feel many powerful emotions as a result of experiencing the story. One reason many readers loved the novel was because it was epistolary in fashion. As opposed to feeling as if the action has already happened, the epistolary novel made readers feel as if they were a part of the action. When they read each letter, it felt as if they were experiencing the gripping story firsthand. Although the novel was loved by some, many other readers were upset with Richardson after he tortured Clarissa so thoroughly. Aside from the fact that the novel was incredibly sad, he was seen as both playing out his own fantasies and being heartless. For example, the novel consists of many moments where Clarissa is greatly abused. At one point, she is raped by the astoundingly evil antagonist, Lovelace, and is damaged psychologically as a result. At times, it is easy to see, "...her desperation" (Richardson 277). In addition, her many attempts to receive help and break free from Lovelace's grasp result in failure. For Lovelace, Clarissa is an object he must have, and he makes this clear in stating, "She must be mine, let me do or offer what I will" (Richardson 231). Lastly, she eventually dies after experiencing everything. Experiencing the unfortunate death of such an angelic figure leaves the reader feeling both saddened and angered. Overall, Richardson's novel was a powerful introduction to sensibility for readers, and marked a point in history when the novel of sensibility was on the rise.

Historically, *Clarissa* changed the novel of sensibility. First off, the novel's clever epistolary design allows for readers to feel as if they are a part of the action. Being a part of the action, as opposed to merely reading about it after it has commenced, provokes stronger emotional responses to the material. For example, someone who experiences an earthquake firsthand will be much more shocked by the event than someone hearing about it over the news, long after it has ended. In addition, Richardson's inclusion of an overly ruthless antagonist helps the novel become much more gripping. This fact is easily explained by thinking critically on the issue: if readers want to feel strong emotional responses due to the material, they are not going to read a novel featuring a slightly mean antagonist. A vicious, ruthless and borderline evil antagonist does the job much better. In fact, at times, Lovelace's actions are nearly unbelievable. For example, he states that he, "...pressed with my burning lips the charmingest breast that ever my ravished eyes beheld" (Richardson 272). Additionally, *Clarissa* is interesting, because it begins to explore how sensations and emotions can affect the body. Late in the novel, Clarissa suffers to such an extent that she is psychologically and mentally damaged. The state of her mind is revealed in her many ramblings that she writes on separate papers (Richardson 339-341). Eventually, she passes away as a result of her lengthy and inescapable torture. It seems as if, while sensibility is generally positive, the ability to feel can potentially become lethal. Samuel Richardson's *Clarissa*, with its many traits, changes the novel of sensibility greatly.

The Man of Feeling, by Henry Mackenzie, was published in 1771. It arrived during an age where technology was undergoing drastic improvements, yet also just before romantics began dominating literature. Though the text is short in length, many who read the story thought of it as being masterly. It was host to Mr. Harley, a male protagonist, who deviated from the usual suffering female character. Readers were treated to the then unusual sight of a man weeping and becoming emotional. One such time occurs towards the end of the novel when Mr. Harley confesses his love to the love of his life. After doing so, he promptly passes away due to the sheer emotion stemming from the situation. At one point, after hearing news of Miss Walton's marriage plans, he shows the reader how much he cares by exclaiming, "Why, it mayn't be true, Sir" (Mackenzie 79). Though many readers had witnessed such strong emotion in other novels before, they had rarely ever read of a man being the one filled with emotion.

The Man of Feeling changed the novel of sensibility a great amount. First, it provided readers with an emotional male as opposed to female. With a man experiencing such feelings, many readers differed in their opinions of the text. A portion of readers saw a man being the emotional protagonist as an improvement and a breath of fresh air for the genre. However, many others were largely opposed to the idea of a sensitive male character. This kind of character put a man's masculinity into question, and created opposition to the book. Though, overall, the book was well received by critics. Another way this novel of sensibility changed the genre was by having the protagonist being tortured by love, as opposed to some sort of ruthless antagonist. Mr. Harley truly loves a woman he cannot obtain, and is tormented by this fact throughout the novel. This fact greatly contrasts *Clarissa*, which features a helpless female being tortured by the antagonist, Lovelace. In *The Man of Feeling*, it is merely love that Mr. Harley desires. Additionally, the novel confirms that emotions and sensations affect the body. In the end of the novel, Mr. Harley eventually dies after steadily declining in terms of health.. At last, he is unable to remain in good health while dealing with such strong emotions. With his love at his deathbed, he passes away. This occurs when, "He sighed, and fell back on his seat" (Mackenzie 96). The ending echoes the ending of *Clarissa*, with the protagonist feeling physical pain due to strong emotional distress. *The Man of Feeling* changes the novel of sensibility in a number of ways, leading some readers to question the typical elements of a novel of sensibility.

Jane Austen's *Sense and Sensibility* was published in 1811, and was extremely well received by readers. It was also written in epistolary form, and allowed readers to feel as if they were witnessing the experience first hand. The novel consisted of two sisters, Elinor and Marianne, who differed greatly in terms of emotion. Elinor is the extremely reserved sister who finds herself bottling up her emotions, and hiding her feelings. While many others find her to be too cold and impersonal for their liking, she is truly full of emotion. However, this emotion is generally kept secret, and she finds herself putting more effort into everyone else's issues. Even though she has strong feelings for Edward, much of the feelings never come out and go undelivered. Contrasting Elinor is Marianne, who is usually overly emotional. Moreover, she always expresses herself more easily than her sister, Elinor. In addition, her eagerness to express her emotions proves to be just as problematic as Elinor's reluctance to show her emotions. Towards the end of the novel, Marianne begins to reason with herself and see Elinor's behavior as admirable. *Sense and Sensibility* provides for two emotionally opposite characters who eventually find the others actions to be somewhat reasonable.

The journey of both sisters is gripping, complex and full of emotional differences. To begin the journey, Elinor is always reserved and respectful. She finds herself worrying about her family's affairs, while pushing her own aside. Though she feels great emotion, passion and desire inside, she fails to show it. In time, she finds herself falling in love with Edward Ferrars, but is unable to pursue him. Instead, she sees her love for him as taking second place in terms of priority. This event proves to be problematic as she is unable to express herself and truly chase after Edward in an efficient manner. Rather, she is left dealing with her family's problems and her thirst for true love goes unquenched. Furthermore, while many people find her to be cold and impersonal, she is actually just as human as anyone else. She feels strong emotions, passion and desires. Unfortunately, her need to be extremely reserved and restrained is what keeps her from pursuing her love interest. One moment where her reserved nature shows occurs when Marianne is visibly stricken with grief, but she watches, "...without saying a word..." (Austen 173). The complete opposite of Marianne, Elinor's reserved nature leads to numerous problems as she is unable to live in an emotionally freeing manner.

Marianne's journey is equally as complex as her sister's. She is extremely emotional, and is generally unable to contain herself. This occurs when she is, "...stretched out on the bed, almost choaked by grief" (Austen

173). Also, her interest in men is largely reflective of her character as she enjoys the company of overly romantic and enthusiastic men. For example, two men appear to take interest in Marianne as a lover. The first, Colonel Brandon, is very calm and reserved. Though he would most likely make for a halfway decent lover, she is uninterested. Instead, she takes interest in the emotional Mr. Willoughby. Eventually, after much progression, Marianne finds herself desiring to be like her sister. She wishes to be more reserved, and finds her sister's once questionable personality to be admirable. In conclusion, with both main characters contrasting each other to such a large extent, *Sense and Sensibility* provides readers with a unique view of emotion.

Jane Austen's *Sense and Sensibility* did quite a bit for the novel of sensibility. Primarily, it provided readers with a chance to directly compare and contrast reserved and emotional characters. The reader is able to view the actions of Marianne, who is highly emotional. Also, the reader is able to contrast her actions with Elinor's generally reserved personality. As a result, readers can directly compare the two and find benefits and faults in both. In *The Man of Feeling* and *Clarissa*, there is only an emotional protagonist. While there is nothing wrong with such a setup, it is still unable to give readers the chance to view the two opposites in one novel. Additionally, can figure out the pros and cons of either side of emotion after contrasting and comparing the two. Some may feel as if leading a more reserved life is ideal, and provides for a better way of living. On the contrary, others may feel as if the bottling up of emotions is harmful. Perhaps those strong emotions mean something, and they serve a purpose. Maybe those many emotions, after being restrained and contained, could potentially be harmful. Whatever the reader's decision, it is important to note that *Sense and Sensibility* provides for both a lack of and an extreme amount of emotion. Such a feature in two main characters was unheard of before the novel was published, and was never the focus.

Jane Austen's *Sense and Sensibility* compares to other novels of sensibility in a number of ways. It is similar in the idea that sensations can affect the body. This concept was explored lightly in the novel, but explored greatly in both *Clarissa* and *The Man of Feeling*. Though neither Marianne nor Elinor pass away due to feeling extreme emotion, they seem to be affected by their experiences. Additionally, the novel relates to other novels of sensibility as it is based around love and relationships with the opposite sex. Henry Mackenzie's *The Man of Feeling* is host to a man who passes away due to feeling extreme emotion resulting from failed love. *Clarissa* also relates as the entire novel revolves around the relationship between Lovelace and Clarissa. Though the relationship is not exactly ideal, it certainly relates to the relationships sought by both Elinor and Marianne. Another way the novel relates to others is the fact that most everyone is wealthy. Though Lovelace is not exactly wealthy beyond measure, even he is not too bad off. In fact, no main character discussed is without moderate amounts of money. None of the three novels of sensibility explored is host to an extremely poor antagonist or protagonist. Lastly, *Sense and Sensibility* relates to other novels of sensibility, because it promotes the idea that feeling too much emotion and experiencing too many sensations can be harmful in numerous ways. Marianne and Elinor's extreme emotion is certainly unhelpful at times, and this fact relates to Mr. Harley and Clarissa's unfortunate outcome. Though the novel is unique in many ways, it compares to other novels of sensibility to a great extent.

While *Sense and Sensibility* compares to other novels of sensibility quite a bit, it is also different in a number of ways, First, the novel establishes a sort of happy medium between both extremes of emotion. Though this was not the authorial intention, it happens as readers are able to judge both extremes. There are certainly benefits and problems with being too emotional or too reserved, and the novel exposes them. Luckily, after experiencing the many events in *Sense and Sensibility*, the reader is able to distinguish what is a safe medium between the two extremes. Being too reserved leads to the restraining of potentially beneficial emotions, and being too emotional can provide for a weak image. *Sense and Sensibility*'s very inclusion of two main characters who represent both sides of feeling also contrasts other novels of sensibility. Up until the novel was released, novels of sensibility were primarily focused on one character. However, Jane Austen's novel follows the progression of both Marianne and Elinor, rendering the story unique and thought provoking. In addition, there is no ruthless antagonist in the story. The story stays focused on the relationships of Elinor and Marianne with their love interests. Lastly, the novel does not end with death being the result of extreme emotion. Unlike *Clarissa* and *The Man of Feeling*, which feature Clarissa and Mr. Harley dying, this novel does not resort to such an outcome. Instead, both sisters find unique solutions to their situations, and move carry on with their lives. In conclusion, while *Sense and Sensibility* is similar to other novels of sensibility in many ways, it is host to numerous differences.

With the arrival of the Age of Sensibility came the realization of just how important sensations and emotions were. Experiencing said emotions through literature became common, and many novels of sensibility were published. Though Samuel Richardson's *Clarissa* and Henry Mackenzie's *The Man of Feeling* proved to be great works of the genre, Jane Austen's *Sense and Sensibility* provided the reader with a unique experience. The novel is host to extreme emotion, and allows readers to test their own ability to feel emotions and sensations while reading particularly gripping texts.

SOURCES

Austen, Jane. *Sense and Sensibility*. Ed. Tony Tanner. New York: Penguin Books, 1995.

Mackenzie, Henry. *The Man of Feeling*. Ed. Brian Vickers. New York: Oxford University Press,1987.

Richardson, Samuel. *Clarissa*. New York: New American Library, 2005.

"Sensibility." Merriam-Webster Online Dictionary. 2009. Merriam-Webster Online. 15 Dec. 2009.

10. Modern Masculinity and the Use of Groups and Structured Dominance for Power

The Social Bonding of Man

Masculinity and its many definitions are a literary gray area. While there are standard understandings of masculinity which stem from stereotypes and classical understandings of the word, contemporary masculinity is not so easily defined. A concrete definition is difficult to place, because masculinity is in a constant state of change. Some of these changes may be rapid and chaotic, and others may last over centuries of time. Adding their own theories on masculinity to the ever-growing field of masculine studies are David Collinson, Jeff Hearn and Kaja Silverman. Collinson and Hearn's essay "Naming Men as Men" focuses on the power of groups as well as the prevalence of structured and institutionalized dominance. Shifting focus, Silverman's essay "Masochism and Male Subjectivity" explores alternate meanings behind male violence and masochistic behavior. Together, these theorists allow for improved understandings of masculinity studies as well as various texts due to their offering of new or altered perspectives.

Even though women in select first world countries have made strides within recent decades, male dominance is still an institutionalized, organized and well structured force. In David Collinson and Jeff Hearn's essay "Naming Men as Men" the subject of modern male dominance is explored. Their focuses are on how masculinity relies on groups for power, the dangers of groups, masculinity's identity within itself and how men implement a strategic and well structured resistance against women and their rise in power. Their proposed theory reacts against the entry level understanding of gender studies which claims for women to have risen in power and men to have declined. Their research shows how men still use groups for power, exclude others, and label anyone outside of their way of thinking as "inferior." Differences in

93

power as a result of gender are still thriving in contemporary society. In addition to finding information, Collinson and Hearn arrive at a number of questions to ask when examining a text: should unities or differences be the focus of analyses, and how are they related? Their essay also questions the prominence of structured and organized dominance, and where it can be found within the text. He then stresses, "we would argue for the need to examine *both* the unities and differences between men and masculinities as well as their interrelations" (153). Through the investigation of both sides of the issue, more is understood about the issue and the numerous complexities by which it is surrounded. Collinson further explains that "by examining these processes *simultaneously*, we can develop a deeper understanding of the gendered power relations of organization, the conditions, processes and consequences of their reproduction and how they could be resisted and transformed" (153). Focusing on not just dominant masculinity, but also its less popular forms allows for an exhaustive yet thorough understanding of male dominance in contemporary society. After applying Collinson and Hearn's theories to a text in an attempt to better understand present day masculinities, readers and viewers alike are potentially able to both view dominance in a new light and ask new questions.

While masculinity may appear to be a concrete and stable issue, it is often subject to change. Collinson explains this issue in stating, "it is important to acknowledge the way in which masculinities can change over time, could be shaped by underlying ambiguities and uncertainties, may differ according to class, age, culture and ethnicity etc" (153). Masculinity experiences changes both fast and slow, and sometimes undergoes change that lasts for generations. Examples of this are found in hairstyles, physical fitness and social standing. Male hairstyles often change frequently, greatly differing from one decade to the next; masculinity defined by physical fitness is always in a slow moving state of change, and men have often found themselves in positions of power and dominance in society throughout time.

Due to frequent changes and the difference they bring, it is difficult to determine where to focus when evaluating masculinity.

Acknowledging division, Collinson explores the issue of differing masculinities and their effects. He stresses that the focus on, "difference ought not to degenerate into a diversified pluralism that gives insufficient attention to structured patterns of gendered power, control and inequality" (153). In other words, throughout the many masculinities and their complex workings, it is theorized that perhaps masculinity is not simply about inequality and power as a result of gender. However, he does entertain the other side of the argument. He explains the opposing viewpoint in stating, "a focus on multiple masculinities should not 'deflect attention from the consistency of men's domination of women at systematic and organizational levels, from the continuation of materials, structured inequalities and power imbalances between the sexes'" (153). While it is important to focus on and explore masculinity as a standalone issue, it is also potentially equally as important to focus on masculinity in relation to women. Examining the structure of male dominance reveals, "asymmetrical relations of power between men and women" (153). This issue is still quite important and persists today, despite the many decades of progress by women's rights groups. Collinson hypothesizes that this lingering imbalance between the two sexes is a result of, "structured domination" (153). Meaning that, according to Collinson and Hearn, whatever male dominance remains is deliberate as opposed to by chance. The presence of not simply domination and power, but structured domination and power indicates a deliberate effort to remain in control. While theorists and rights activists may differ in their opinion on how best to focus on masculinity, both sides provide for both crucial and insightful research.

Much of male dominance in contemporary society is thought to stem from power in groups. Collinson explains how, "men's power in organizations is maintained through their unification and identification with each other" (153). Strength in numbers helps maintain dominance in various ways, such as resources and validation. With many men helping maintain dominance, it is clear that more resources are being used for the effort. Simply enough, the more men targeting the same goal, the better the results. Also, men functioning in groups can validate their motives and opinions by constantly reinforcing themselves. A man acting out on his own may potentially stop to question himself, whereas a group of men are more likely to stay united in their beliefs and actions. In addition, Collinson further examines men in groups, stating, "men are frequently united, though not necessarily consciously, by dominant sexuality, violence and potential violence, social and economic privilege, political power, shared concerns and interests and culturally based values" (153). Whether it is a conscious effort to stay grouped or not, men often find themselves together and united due to their similarities. For example, many men are similar in that political power tends to historically lean in their favor. Also, men have typically earned more money than women throughout history. Similarities help bind men together and unite them in their similar interests and experiences.

On the topic of institutionalized and structured dominance, Collinson and Hearn explore how men use tactics to weaken women. Collinson finds that equal opportunity exists to allow men to help other men, and to help, "deny that gender inequalities continue to exist" (155). Such a program allows men to act as if gender inequality is a thing of the past, but instead it allows for it to continue while keeping many blind to the issue. He further notes how, "such programmes not only unite men, but also individualize and divide women" (155). Relating directly to the idea that there is strength in numbers and groups for men, dividing and individualizing is a key tactic used to weaken women. Similar to the old saying, "united we stand, divided we fall," women are much easier to oppress if they remain broken up and disallowed from unifying. At its worst, structured dominance is a prevailing issue that allows for both the control of women and long lasting power of men.

Unfortunately for men, using groups and large numbers for power also has its downsides. Collinson believes that "the idea of a unity of men is *also* problematic" (154). His findings support the idea that groups tend to have a major weakness: exclusion. There is evidence for, "white heterosexual able-bodied men [excluding] other kinds of men" (154). In fact, according to Collinson, it "remains a major issue" (154). While it is clear that men bound in groups often results in power, the exclusion of select varieties of men has the potential to create controversy. With this issue being detected and recognized, he states, "these differences must be examined" (154). According to Collinson, it is important to analyze how these "unities *and* differences between men and masculinities" overlap (154). With the existence of so many differing masculinities, the best way to understand contemporary masculinity as a whole is by investigating their numerous similarities and differences. Only then are the powers and weaknesses of masculinity understood to the fullest possible extent.

In conclusion, Collinson and Hearn wrap up their investigation of structured masculinity on a reflective note. The essay mentions how, "up to now, there has been far more attention given to the implication of gender class analysis for women than for men" (154). While men have often been the focus of history, masculinity itself is still a relatively new subject on which to focus. Moderate amounts of research have been done to illustrate how men remain dominant and keep others out of power. For example, Collinson uses the damaging presence of, "institutional and cultural barriers to womens 'progress'" (153-154). The fact that men often operate in well organized groups in order to keep women weak reveals the real stranglehold dominant men have on others. Such groups and, "organizations are dominated by a group that has the power to define all other groups as inferior" (154). Such actions are done to ensure that male dominance will last, and that no other opposing parties may rise to a threatening level of power and influence. Additionally, he suggests "that the increasing emphasis on multiplicity and differentiation needs to be combined with a consideration of men's unites and their interrelations." (155). Even though both sides have been explored: one viewing masculinity as a single issue and the other viewing it in relation to women and even other factions within itself, it is best to attempt to see masculinity in both ways. Collinson feels that this would allow for the most complete understanding of contemporary masculinity and its issues.

In Kaja Silverman's "Masochism and Male Subjectivity," she reacts to Freudian gender theory and explores physical abuse and its various understandings. She pushes whoever examines a text to answer the question, "what is it precisely that the male masochist displays, and what are the consequences of this self-exposure?" (36). Such a question applies directly to Chuck Palahniuk's *Fight Club*, due to physical violence being at its center. According to Silverman, it is important to explore texts and attempt to find instances of male masochistic behavior, as well the consequences of putting on such a display. On one hand, such behavior can be regarded as liberating, but on the other hand, it can say more about the man than originally intended.

The problems faced by men in contemporary society are relatively easy to comprehend, yet they are difficult to truly understand. Silverman explains this belief further, noting how, "when a woman doesn't identify with a classically female position, she is expected to identify with a classically male one" (34). However, though she can identify with a classically male position after failing to identify with a stereotypically female one, she is unable to fully understand what it means to be a man. Silverman furthers her idea, stating, "the girl's identification with the male position does not imply an identification with activity" (34). In other words, by using fantasy, she can take on the role of a man without becoming active in a masculine way. What results from both pretending to be masculine and attempting to become a man is a paper thin understanding of male identity. According to Silverman, this lack of understanding suggests that understanding masculine identity is out of the question for women, even if they have already failed at identifying with classically female positions.

Silverman's focus on masochism and the meanings surrounding

98

physical violence stems largely from Sigmund Freud. The sight of physical violence in stereotypical masculinity and films such as *Fight Club* suggests the presence of what Freud called "the beating fantasy." First mentioned by Freud after observing the behavioral issues found in women, the beating fantasy has slowly crept its way into masculine studies. According to Silverman, men sometimes insert, "themselves in the masculine version of the beating fantasy" (34). Examples of this are found in *Fight Club* and numerous other Hollywood films where physical violence and fighting are core issues. What is less known is the meaning behind the masochistic practice, and how it actually relates to femininity. Given that Freud first found evidence of the beating fantasy in women, Silverman believes the male masochistic version of this behavior to suggest a desire to become feminine. She explains that "the male subject thus secures access to femininity through identification with the mother" (34). Through being beaten and suffering physical pain, men are apparently able to relate and identify with their mothers who may have also been subjected to this treatment. Oftentimes, she notes, the focus on behalf of the male subjects is centered around, "pain and humiliation" (36). In addition to the beating fantasy, she argues that "some effort is made to conceal the *homosexual* content of the conscious fantasy," and yet "no corresponding attempt is made to hide its *masochistic* content" (35). She feels that this effort to hide certain aspects of masochism displays what is acceptable and unacceptable within the behavior. For example, in *Fight Club* the narrator and his friend Tyler Durden often visit their underground boxing clubs in order to experience pain and receive physical abuse. While it is debated that the homosocial nature of the two characters goes beyond male-centered friendship and extends into homosexuality, there is no definitive proof within the film. In other words, if there is homosexual content in the film, it is well hidden. This conscious effort being made to hide or disguise homosexuality illuminates the taboos within the behavior. However, on the other hand, the masochistic content of *Fight Club* is never hidden and remains blatantly present throughout the film. At face value, the practice itself may be considered socially unacceptable, but there is even further meaning surrounding certain practices that suggest there are rights and wrongs within the behavior. The practice of purposely experiencing pain is not a simple issue, and within it are many meanings and understandings.

The aforementioned theories by Silverman and Collinson are able to be applied to various texts. Briefly examining *Fight Club* through the lenses provided by the theorists allows for a new understanding of the film. For example, Collinson focuses on the reliance on groups by men and how they are a source of control and power. In Palahniuk's *Fight Club*, the narrator and his alter ego Tyler Durden form a group based around physical violence and masochistic behavior. After establishing their underground boxing club, they are able to form rules and set guidelines for living. Their power and influence are greatly expanded after unifying. In fact, though the men in the film act violently and subject themselves to pain just as Silverman pointed out, the presence of groups precedes the formation of Fight Club. Early in the film, the narrator attends various support groups in order to cry; a requirement for temporarily curing his troublesome insomnia. The reliance on groups for power and control is not necessarily always violent in nature and can be for achieving something as simple as a good night's sleep. Applying Silverman and Collinson's personal theories on masculinity to texts provides for alternate meanings and potentially better understandings through new perspectives.

Masculinity studies owes its modern existence to the numerous theorists who attempt to further define it. With its nearly impossible to define identity, fluid nature and application to numerous academic studies, masculinity studies is often the subject of investigation and close examination. In this case, masochistic behavioral practices as well as the reliance on groups and structured dominance for power are studied by Silverman, Collinson and Hearn respectively. Their investigations of masculinity and how it presents itself in contemporary society allow new information to be gathered. Literary theorists and their work provide others with improved understandings of masculine studies and numerous texts thanks to their offering of modified perspectives.

SOURCES

Silverman, Kaja. "Masochism and Male Subjectivity." *The Masculinity Studies Reader*. Rachel Adams and David Savran, eds. Malden, Massachusetts: Blackwell Publishers, 2002. 21-40. Print.

Collinson, David and Jeff Hearn. "Naming Men as Men." *The Masculinities Reader*. Ed. Stephen Whitehead. Malden, Massachusetts: Polity Press, 2001. 144-169. Print.

11. A Child of His Times: Immanuel Kant and Enlightenment

Man as Closed-Minded

It is often the case that the thinkers of yesteryear appear to be immortalized in their words. Locked safely in the past, it would seem that the messages of these thinkers and their meanings are outside of the realm of reinterpretation. However, thanks to the modern literary approach known as New Historicism, this assumption is not true at all. In actuality, history and its thinkers are never set in stone and outside of reexamination. As definitions, morals and meanings all change with the times, historical figures are placed back under the microscope. One such historical figure is the Enlightenment Era philosopher Immanuel Kant, who often wrote on his ideas of what it means to be enlightened, maturation, knowledge and ignorance. The particular work in question is "An Answer to the Question: What is Enlightenment?" Written in 1784, the brief text explores the definition of enlightenment itself and how to achieve it. While the text appears to be crafted innocently enough, present day interpreter Robert Bernasconi argues otherwise. In his essay, "Will the Real Kant Please Stand Up?" he examines racist elements of the philosopher's piece. Despite the fact that he arrives at the conclusion that Kant was racist in his writings, the topics of self-awareness and ignorance must be investigated in order to better understand from where it is Kant was coming. This process works in opposition to simply labeling him through the lens of a person reading over two hundred years in the future.

The Age of Enlightenment was a supposed coming of consciousness for the people of the world, but this idea is debatable. It is difficult to believe the aforementioned definition to be true when certain people were not even conscious of themselves and their opinions. Of the prominent figures in Western philosophy during the time is Immanuel Kant, who wrote "An Answer to the Question: What is Enlightenment?" A primary point in achieving enlightenment was for man to venture from out of the darkness, and lift the veil that is self-imposed and intentional immaturity. Kant himself explains how, "Enlightenment is man's emergence from his self-imposed immaturity" (Kant). The idea that the immaturity from which humans were suffering was self-imposed is striking, because it suggests that humans are the only things holding humans back from excelling. It suggests that humans are capable of so much more, and they only need to rise up in terms of consciousness to achieve that sought-after state of enlightenment. However, while his initial description of enlightenment appears to be innocent enough, there are immediate issues that arise soon after.

Given the imperialism of the time, Kant's own description of enlightenment can be interpreted as racist. In his description of immaturity, he explains it as, "the inability to use one's understanding without guidance from another" (Kant). According to those such as Bernasconi, this could mean so much more than initially thought. The key part of the sentence coming under question is, "without guidance from another." Considering the time period and the intricacies behind colonialism, stating that true enlightenment could only be gained when the achievement of a higher understanding is done without help from others is close to crossing a thin line. Supplementing this statement is Kant's further explanation, "This immaturity is self-imposed when its cause lies not in lack of understanding, but in lack of resolve and courage to use it without guidance from another" (Kant). Again, there is an emphasis on needing to have someone else help, and what that means within the grand picture of enlightenment. Whether the interpretation is correct or incorrect, statements such as these appear to be racist in the eyes of present day readers. Given the imperialistic nature of the moment, and how all others ranging from Eastern Asians to Africans were thought to be lesser beings, the statements made by Kant seem to fit the mold: there is a sense of superiority, the lack of understanding of how others could be so ignorant in comparison to one's own culture, and the idea that other cultures need to be fixed for

103

whatever reason, as if they are inherently broken. In the mind of a modern reader, especially one who is sensitive towards civil issues such as these, the writings of Kant seem to be racist. Furthermore, this repeated reference to "alien guidance," and how it removes them from a "lifelong immaturity" are troubling (Kant). The idea pushed by Kant is that it is not the people themselves who are wrong, it is just their "nature" (Kant). These sorts of statements are unmistakably laced with a sense of superiority, as if all others are outside the intelligence of their European oppressors.

Whether it is the glaringly obvious superiority complexes of select writers, or plain racism, some researchers feel as if these elements are common within Western texts. In the text titled "Will the Real Kant Please Stand Up?" issues such as racism and superiority are explored by Robert Bernasconi. He feels as if Western philosophy is riddled with racism, and points to how it is indicative of the times. He explains, "I will be referring to the racism that we often find in the texts of some of the most eminent figures of the history of Western philosophy" (Bernasconi 13). In other words, according to him, racism has been a common occurrence in the world of Western thinking for ages. For one, he feels as if it is largely ignored. Bernasconi states, "the focus of this article is not so much on their racism, but on our ways of addressing it, or, more often, our ways of not addressing it" (13). While the topic of Western racism is important, the key reason for crafting his text is to show that these instances go unaddressed. Additionally, Bernasconi then ponders if ignoring the racism of others is a form of racism all by itself. He explains, "My question is whether there is not an institutional racism within contemporary philosophy that emerges in our tendency to ignore or otherwise play down their racism while we celebrate their principles" (13). Unlike others who have shied away from approaching the racism of prominent figures, Bernasconi feels as if the only option is to pursue it. If not for the sake of curiosity, then for the sake of better understanding the major thinkers whose ideas influenced the world. He states that "we should make their racism a further reason to interrogate them"

(13). Bernasconi feels as if this is the correct course of action, because, "they were unquestionably major philosophers whose impact lives on outside the academy as well as in it" (13). With his identification of Kant's racist remarks stems the larger question of how such a topic should be approached.

Immediately after pointing out the racist remarks made by Western philosophers, Bernasconi delves deeper into how to deal with such a delicate subject. While he wonders, "how should we address the racism of Locke and Kant?" what drives him is the larger question of, "how the racism of these thinkers relates to their philosophy" (13). Once identified, it is important to realize that their racist beliefs affect their very philosophies. However, despite these claims of racism, could it be that writers such as Kant, "simply shared the assumptions of the time?" (14). It could be the case that Kant's views and morals coexisted with racist thoughts.

Despite the fact that Kant's writings had racist elements, he was undoubtedly a product of the times and the understandings of the people. Like Bernasconi himself states, it would appear that racism is, "no more than a surface feature of a philosophy" (15). The very openness of Kant in his writings suggests that there was a, "freedom from racism," or rather, charges of racism (17). The reason for this is the simple fact that, aside from nationalism, such beliefs were lodged into the minds of the people during this time period (19). When out exploring the world and conquering lands with valuable resources, rulers and commanders alike knew the value of having an inspired people behind them with a sense of being inherently better than others outside of the empire. The result was a boost in morale, and a sense of order and control. Another difficult aspect of this situation is the fact that many of the oppressors and their allies were totally ignorant of the fact that their opinions of others were not their own. The ignorance of these planted, engineered opinions is somewhat ironic given the topic of the enlightenment. In addition, Bernasconi may be partially correct in suggesting that these sorts of writings are one of racism's last, "hiding places," but it may be the simple fact that people recognize obviously outdated ways of thinking from afar (17).

Bernasconi incorrectly states that modern society is afraid of, "saying certain things," and is afraid of pointing out, "racial inequalities," but this could not be further from the truth, especially given the politically correct environment that has been constructed. Out of any time period in society, the people of the present day West would most likely be the first to point out the racism of another. However, given the writer and the time period of his compositions, the entire process seems to be needless. Pointing out the superiority complex of an imperial citizen, whether it is racially driven or not, is a needless process. Similar to Shakespeare's antisemitism, or Aristotle's belief that women were lesser citizens, the opinions of Kant in relation to enlightenment are noticeably outdated and do not need investigation. As Bernasconi himself states midway through his text, Kant was a, "child of his time" (19). He was a product of his environment and those who were in control of information at the time.

In order to better understand from where writers such as Kant were coming, it is important to examine their surroundings and the common beliefs shared at the time. During the Age of Enlightenment, Europe's reach and resulting influence was spreading throughout the globe. With that being said, it is no wonder some of Kant's writings stressed that enlightenment was achieved only through a guidance-free removal of immaturity. After all, it is what the empires of Europe were able to achieve. At least, in the eyes of Europe. Yet, for the rest of the world, their enlightenment was at the hands of Western civilization. In other words, even though other cultures were removed from the blinding darkness of ignorance, it is because they received help that they are inferior. Their enlightenment had "alien" help. In conclusion, the writings of Kant and other Western philosophers are indeed racist at times, but they are products of the time period and its imperialistic nature. These writings were host to beliefs that were engrained in the minds of the people. As far as historicism goes, it is possible to examine many similar instances: look no further than the opinions of the Hitler Youth or the participants of the October Revolution. Closed circuited, tight-knit groups of people reinforcing and strengthening their own opinions leads to the sort of ignorance witnessed in the writings of Kant and other Western thinkers: a level of closed-mindedness and brainwashing that has permeated so deeply, that even a writer composing a piece on ignorance is wholly unaware of the ignorance found within his very own text.

SOURCES

Bernasconi, Robert. "Will the Real Kant Please Stand Up? The challenge of Enlightenment racism to the study of the history of philosophy." *Radical Philosophy* 117 (2003): 13-22. Web.

Kant, Immanuel. "An Answer to the Question: What is Enlightenment?" 1784. Hosted at University of Pennsylvania. Retrieved 3.2.12. Web.

12. Power as Defined by Relationships With Men

Associations of Man

Power is defined in numerous ways. In Shakespeare's many plays, there are several male figures of power, and they are all subject to unique conditions. However, it is important to examine the circumstances surrounding women's power. Miranda has very little strength in *The Tempest* as she is literally controlled and put to sleep. Desdemona, from *Othello*, is in a position of power due to her marriage with Othello, but can never actually exercises it. *Richard III*'s Anne is easily coerced into liking the man who recently murdered her husband, displaying her lack of mental power. Emilia's defiance in *Othello* defines her inner strength. Lastly, Nerissa, Jessica and Portia from *The Merchant of Venice* all act out in unusual ways, displaying their numerous strengths. After examining the power of these several women in Shakespeare's plays, it is possible that their strength is defined only by their relationships with the men around them.

One of the weakest of Shakespeare's characters is Miranda from *The Tempest*. She is a young and fortunate girl who has escaped persecution with her father. Although her initial troubles seem to be over, there are plenty more on behalf of her father to fill the void. Since escaping, she lives with her father on a moderately sized and mostly uninhabited island. Aside from sharing the island with their servant, Caliban, they remain in solitude. Moreover, with just her and her father on the island, he is able to fully control her in an overbearing and unrestricted manner.

Miranda ranks as being very weak, due to her unbelievable relationship with her father, Prospero. Early on in the play, her father decides that it is best for her to begin sleeping. Without asking or suggesting to her that she sleeps, he tells her, "Thou art inclined to sleep" (*The Tempest* 1. 2. 185). Within a short moment, she falls fast to sleep. This moment in the play is important, because it demonstrates his complete control over her. Unlike

108

most cases of abuse and male dominance, she is literally controlled. Being commanded to sleep, told to sleep and asked to sleep all rank far above this action, because there is an option. Here, she is made into a slave as there is no chance for opposition. As a result, she comes across as being less than human, because she is controlled to such a full extent. For a good portion of the play, Miranda engages, "...in what is, by most informed standards, naïve, if not absurd, behavior" (Petry 29). Without question, Miranda is unfortunately the epitome of objectification due her father's full and complete control over her body.

Due to her interactions with men, Desdemona from Shakespeare's *Othello* reveals herself to be quite weak. David Berkeley states that "...Desdemona never employs wit in her relations with Othello..." (Berkeley 235). For example, she is taken in by Othello's stories, and that is how she comes to admire him. She loves his stories of, "...battles sieges, [and] fortunes" (*Othello* 1. 3. 132). Winning her over with words demonstrates how easily coerced she is. Although she may be his wife and in a position of power, she rarely exercises any sort of strength. Later in the play, Iago tells Othello lies about her, and they are instantly believed. Othello focuses on how she may have interrupted the bloodline, and does not trust Desdemona anymore. He does not seem to care about, "...Desdemona's innocence and virtue..." (Ranald 128). Throughout the play, she ventures from having little power to being powerless as Othello murders her in her room. Unfortunately, her power was defined by another man for the duration of the play, and she was unable to strengthen herself in a significant manner.

Anne, from Shakespeare's *Richard III*, reveals herself to be quite weak. Early in the novel, it is explained that Richard has killed Anne's former love. Understandably, Anne becomes angry with Richard. Though, after just a short period of time and some conversation, Richard coerces Anne into loving him. He explains that he merely killed her former husband out of love for her, and she ends up feeling flattered. In addition, she then goes as far as to blame herself for the murders. Her reasoning is that Richard murdered out of love for her, so it must ultimately be her fault. As unbelievable as it seems, she ends up admiring Richard by the end of the conversation (*Richard III* 1. 2.). What is even more astonishing than Anne's interest in Richard is that he is merely wooing her out of sport. Even he cannot believe that she is beginning to love him. Furthermore, it is because of Anne's thoughtless actions when dealing with Richard that she reveals herself to be unintelligent and easily manipulated. Given the circumstances, this overly easy manipulation seems to be accompanied by weakness in mind.

Emilia's relationship with powerful men in *Othello* displays her inner strength. For example, some of the time she makes an appearance during the play, she argues with Iago. At one point she tells Iago, "Do not you chide. I have a thing for you," and begins quarreling with him over the handkerchief (*Othello* 3. 3. 318). When contrasted with Othello's dominance over Desdemona, Emilia begins to stand out as an exceptional woman. Rather than falling into society's mold for females, she tends to disapprove of her husband and his wicked actions. During this time period, such a rebellious action was worthy of a hefty scolding, a beating or worse depending on the gravity of the situation. While she in no way controls the relationship, she is brave for speaking back to her husband. Therefore, she must be strong, because such bravery requires strength.

Emilia's power is defined by her relationship with Othello as well. Late in the play, Emilia visits the room of Desdemona, but does not know that she has been murdered. As Desdemona's primary caretaker, she wishes to enter the bedroom and visit, but Othello greets her. Combining her fine tuned perception and intelligence, she notices that something is not right about the situation or Othello's behavior. Othello demands that she leaves him alone, but she refuses. She does not accept being driven away, and decides to enter the room. Additionally, as if defying the strong Othello was not enough, she decides to call for help. Emilia yells out, "Help, help, ho, help! O lady, speak again!" (*Othello* 5. 2. 124). These two actions in rapid succession could have spelled doom for her as she was not only going against Othello's

orders, but also revealing a gruesome scene. She could have been threatened, hurt, or even killed as a result of her actions. However, she was not killed by Othello, and her bravery is the cause for the gruesome scene being revealed. Similar to defying Iago, her actions required great amounts of bravery. Furthermore, the bravery behind her actions stems from her immense strength.

Though Nerissa, from *The Merchant of Venice*, is not in a position of power, her interaction with men displays her as being powerful. Nerissa is Portia's caretaker and friend, and tends to stick by her side whenever necessary. There are two moments throughout the play where Nerissa demonstrates her power. First, she is able to fool the courts as she disguises herself as a man. Out of the several intelligent men in the audience, nobody notices that she is not really a man. Second, after the case is resolved, she is able to make a fool out of her love, Gratiano (*The Merchant of Venice* 5. 1.). After briefly embarrassing Gratiano after the case, she reveals that she was the young male law clerk. Surprisingly, Gratiano's anger ends at scolding Nerissa for her actions. Though, no matter what the penalty, her power has been demonstrated through her risky actions. She was not only able to fool several intelligent men with her superb disguise, but was also able to fool the very man who confessed his love for her. Above everyone else, he should have been able to see through the disguise and notice her. Conclusively, Nerissa's plan required not simply bravery, but also skill. Helping to conjure up this plan is one thing, but executing it perfectly is another and deserves praise.

Portia also demonstrates her power over men by disguising herself as a skillful and intelligent lawyer. When representing her client, Antonio, she is able to speak fluently and concisely in front of many men. In fact, she is able to speak so well that nobody questions her or becomes remotely suspicious. During the case, Portia is able to outsmart Shylock by toying with the language used in his contract. This is made possible by her, "...highly technical reading of the bond..." (Bilello 12). For example, she makes note that Shylock must remove only skin and no blood, or else he will suffer the consequences (*The Merchant of Venice* 4. 1. 301). Ultimately, her actions in the courtroom, "...spring Antonio loose..." (Halio 59). Out of the many people she outsmarts, Shylock is certainly among the top. Portia is intelligent enough to, "...entrap her victim..." (Halio 59). Moreover, after the case, she preys on another man and convinces Bassanio to give his ring to her. Though Bassanio knows that he must not do this if his love for Portia means anything, he still gives her the ring. These actions set Portia above men in terms of power for a number of reasons. First, she is able to convince many men that she is a male lawyer. Then, she is able to trick her own lover into performing an unintelligent action. However, this action, "...risks the happiness of his union..." (Olson 305). As a result, she makes a joke out of Bassanio as he is easily fooled (*The Merchant of Venice* 5. 1.).

She is also powerful due to a few other reasons. When her father dies, he instructs Portia on how to test the worthiness of men. Portia must arrange three containers, and allow her suitor to choose from one. If the container with her portrait is revealed, her suitor wins her love. Although the process may seem trivial, it ensures that she cannot simply be won over by anyone, regardless of power. The love of Portia requires extreme intelligence, and perhaps the helping hand of luck. Portia is also powerful due to her vast amount of wealth, and the fact that she set the conditions for her marriage with Bassanio. This event occurs directly after Bassanio chooses the right container in front of everyone. She makes it very clear to him that the ring cannot leave his finger, or else her love for him will perish. After reviewing Portia's many striking actions, it is clear that she is above and beyond in terms of power. She was able to fool the courts, outsmart many men, test men for her love and set the conditions for her marriage. The juxtaposition of her actions with the actions of many other female Shakespearean actresses reveals a great deal of contrast as she is incredibly powerful. In conclusion, she displays such a great deal of power over men that she could be seen as an inspiration for many women.

Shylock's daughter, Jessica, is not only the most powerful woman in *The Merchant of Venice*, but also out of any work previously mentioned. In the play, Shylock, "...locks her up as he does his gold, and she betrays him by escaping" (Eggers 330). At one point, she decides that she has had enough with her father's rules, and decides to run off with Lorenzo and his friends. Though, in running off, she does not simply leave her father. In fact, she both greatly disrespects her father in the act, and leaves Judaism as well. Jessica makes it known to the group that she, "...shall be saved by my husband. He hath made me a Christian" (*The Merchant of Venice* 3. 5. 15). It is important to note just how unbelievable these two actions are, especially from a daughter. Up until the point where she leaves, Jessica is seen by some as, "...a figure of conversation" (Metzger 53). To Lorenzo and others, she is seen as a, "...damsel carefully guarded by a jealous father..." (Brown 227). After, she is regarded as being independent. Moreover, for a young daughter to leave her father and break free of his control was a powerful gesture. On top of that, to leave Judaism and join Christianity further added to the chaotic nature of her actions. Though it may be seen as her acting wildly and in an unintelligent manner, her actions are just and necessary. Her ability to break free from her father's constraints and switch religions reveals her as being a very powerful female character.

The many women of Shakespeare's plays vary in terms of strength, and this fact is largely based on their relationships with the men around them. Miranda and Desdemona appear to be weak as they are controlled, ordered around and never fully trusted. Anne displays a lack of mental power as she is convinced by Richard III to love him. As for Emilia, she works against her husband and defies Othello. Her actions show that she is not only defiant, but powerful as well. Lastly, the women of *The Merchant of Venice* prove themselves to be the most powerful of the group. Between them, they are able to trick intelligent minds in court, make fools out of their husbands, disregard a constricting father's orders and abandon a religion. In addition, though power should never only stem from relations with men, it is important to remember that Shakespeare's plays came during a highly sexist period of time. With that being said, Jessica certainly rests above all other women in the examined plays as she is able to exercise her mind, live freely, and make a fool out of her intelligent father.

SOURCES

Berkeley, David. "A Vulgarization of Desdemona." *Studies in English Literature, 1500-1900* 3.2 (1963): 233-239. *JSTOR*. Web. 9 Dec. 2009.

Bilello, Thomas. "Accomplished with What She Lacks: Law, Equity, and Portia's Con." *Law and Literature* 16.1 (2004): 11-32. *JSTOR*. Web. 9 Dec. 2009.

Brown, Beatrice. "Mediaeval Prototypes of Lorenzo and Jessica." *Modern Language Notes* 44.4 (1929): 227-232. *JSTOR*. Web. 9 Dec. 2009.

Eggers, Walter. "Love and Likeness in The Merchant of Venice." *Shakespeare Quarterly* 28.3 (1977): 327-333. *JSTOR*. Web. 9 Dec. 2009.

Halio, Jay. "Portia: Shakespeare's Matlock?" *Cardozo Studies in Law and Literature* 5.1 (1993): 57-64. *JSTOR*. Web. 9 Dec. 2009.

Metzger, Mary Janell. ""Now by My Hood, a Gentle and No Jew": Jessica, The Merchant of Venice, and the Discourse of Early Modern English Identity." *PMLA* 113.1 (1998): 52-63. *JSTOR*. Web. 9 Dec. 2009.

Olson, Trisha. "Pausing upon Portia." *Journal of Law and Religion* 19.2 (2003-2004): 299-330. *JSTOR*. Web. 9 Dec. 2009.

Petry, Alice Hall. "Knowledge in "The Tempest."" *Modern Language Studies* 11.1 (1980-1981): 27-32. *JSTOR*. Web. 9 Dec. 2009.

Ranald, Margaret Loftus. "The Indiscretions of Desdemona." *Shakespeare Quarterly* 14.2 (1963): 127-139. *JSTOR*. Web. 9 Dec. 2009.

Shakespeare, William. *Othello*. Ed. Kim F. Hall. New York: Bedford/St. Martin's, 2007. 45-165.

Shakespeare, William. *Richard III*. Ed. Mark Eccles. New York: Signet Classics, 1998. 3-145.

Shakespeare, William. *The Merchant of Venice*. Ed. M. Lindsay Kaplan. New York: Bedford/St. Martin's, 2002. 25-119.

Shakespeare, William. *The Tempest*. Ed. Gerald Graff and James Phelan. New York: Bedford/St. Martin's, 2009. 10-87.

13. Sir Gawain's Numerous Portrayals in Regards to Masculinity

The Emotional Flexibility of Man

When reading *Sir Gawain and the Green Knight*, it is nearly impossible to finish the tale without noticing issues of gender. Stereotypically, men are strong, intelligent and able to finish tasks with ease. Though, this does not appear to be the absolute case with Sir Gawain. His masculinity is debatable, and numerous events are subject to questioning and debate. Discovering what critics of Sir Gawain and this poem believe is key to further understanding both gender and, in particular, masculinity. Regional differences and differences between tales must be explored, and any gaps found in the research may need to be filled in order to better understand Sir Gawain's masculinity in Arthurian literature.

In "Semantic Social Games and the Game of Life in *Sir Gawain and the Green Knight* and *Arrow-Odd's Saga*" by Jefferey H. Taylor, he notes the importance of Sir Gawain accepting the magic girdle from Lady Bertilak. He believes that it will save his life. With Sir Gawain so easily accepting the magic girdle, it can be contemplated that he is not a typical man. In accepting the gift that may protect his life, he unknowingly shows how weak and frightened he is on the inside. Moreover, Taylor's findings explain how Sir Gawain is rather weak for a man of the time. In truth, such a conclusion that labels a great hero of the time as being weak is usual and does not deviate from the norm. On the contrary, what is unusual about Taylor's article is the idea that Sir Gawain may have not been simply week, but was instead intelligently looking out for his future interests. Taylor explains that "He believes he is going to die, and Lady Bertilak seems to be offering him ample chance at procreation" (Taylor 4). This understanding of their near sexual encounter seems to be unique in explaining the ordeal. As opposed to the common argument that Sir Gawain is weak and Lady Bertilak is a temptress, Taylor suggests that protection and care were the primary elements to their encounter. For example, with Lady Bertilak being perceptive and understanding the situation, she offers Sir Gawain a true chance at protecting his future interests. Sir Gawain, knowing that there is a real chance he may perish in his quest to find the Green Knight, debates within himself about taking Lady Bertilak up on her offer. Though, in the end he does not give in, and his inaction leads to other understandings of the encounter. Perhaps Lady Bertilak was merely trying to help, and Sir Gawain was simply too worried or frightened to take action. Whatever the reasoning behind the decisions made, Taylor stresses that different understandings of the event can drastically change the character's image.

For *Parergon*, Bonnie Lander wrote the article "The Convention of Innocence and *Sir Gawain and the Green Knight*'s Literary Sophisticates" which points out Sir Gawain's weaker moments. When reading *Sir Gawain and the Green Knight*, it is easy to believe that Sir Gawain is a powerful and brave knight. Though, when the events in the poem are closely examined, numerous instances of weakness are present. Lander expands on this, and mentions that "The Green Knight forgives Gawain his weakness..." (Lander 42). This moment in the tale is crucial because it shows not only was Sir Gawain weak at many points within the story, but also that this weakness and lack of masculinity was easily noticed by others. Additionally, Lander then explains the event further in stating, "Gawain follows his refusal of this invitation with a speech intended to defend his cowardly action" (Lander 42). His decision to defend the performing of cowardly deeds greatly contrasts Gowans' article, where she points out his ability to acknowledge his faults as a human being (Gowans 98). This contrast is interesting, because it further adds more ways a single person can be perceived and understood. While some view Sir Gawain to be cowardly and shameful, others view him as being somewhat humble and selfless.

In Linda Gowans' article for *Arthurian Literature* titled "Lamenting or Just Grumbling? Arthur's Nephew Express His Discontent," she examines Sir Gawain's weaknesses and other select elements that make him appear to be feminine in a traditional sense. First off, Gowans stresses the importance of Sir Gawain's attitude towards, "...the hand life has dealt him..." (Gowans 91). In other words, when Sir Gawain suffers from various hardships or other adversity, it is usually his nature to complain in an uncharacteristically feminine fashion. While this statement may appear to be a bit narrow minded at first, it is important to understand that men of this era did not whine and complain in such a fashion. Stereotypically, those actions were dominated by the women. Therefore, with Gowans pointing out Sir Gawain's frequent grumbling and complaining, he is seen in a new light. Instead of conjuring up images and thoughts of a masculine knight, readers find that Sir Gawain is actually quite feminine and weak. In fact, Gowans' is so sure that these actions are meaningful, that she states, "...this information tells us about Gawain's priorities..." (Gowans 91). It would appear that, though Sir Gawain attempts to deal with matters as best as he can, he is unable to continue onward and make progress without whining. On the contrary, this negative portrayal of Sir Gawain is generally limited to specific regions and areas. For example, a large amount of the literature containing Sir Gawain that originated in France portrays him as being weak and insignificant in comparison to English Arthurian literature (Gowans 93). With Sir Gawain's masculinity varying depending on region, it can be concluded that the country of origin must be taken into consideration when making judgments. For example, in the English poem *Sir Gawain and the Green Knight*, Sir Gawain appears to be strong for the most part. Though he does have his moments of weakness, he is able to conclude his quest on a high note. Additionally, Gowans explains how Sir Gawain blamed, "...himself, using terms such as cowardice, reachery and 'untrawthe': much the same faults that he has been anxious to avoid..." (Gowans 98). At this moment, Sir Gawain shows his masculinity not through killing or fighting, but by acknowledging his faults as a human being. In conclusion, ranging from weak to strong, the portrayal of Sir Gawain largely depends on the text's country of origin.

In the article for *Arthuriana* by Corey Owen titled "Patient Lancelot and Impatient Gawain in the *Queste del Saint Graal*," Sir Gawain's negative portrayal reinforces the idea that the text's country of origin is extremely important. With Sir Gawain being featured in a French text, it is nearly to be expected that he is portrayed in a negative light, and that his overall masculinity is damaged. Owen explains, "...whereas both are willing to suffer heroically in order to achieve the quest, only [Lancelot] chooses the sort of suffering that ensures his at least partial success" (Owen 3). In other words, both knights share the traditionally masculine trait of being bold and heroic, but Sir Gawain lacks the mental capacity to utilize those traits efficiently. Sir Gawain's primary fault stems from lacking, "...the virtue of patience..." (Owen 3). Again, it is suggested in the French text that he is simply to hasty, and acts out without fully thinking his future actions through. In addition, it is also expected of masculine and powerful men to be able to complete quests and solve problems. Though, when it comes to Sir Gawain, he is inadequately prepared due to his lack of his patience. Owen explains this further in stating, "...I argue that voluntary suffering in the form of patience is essential to the Grail quest" (Owen 5). Simply put, Sir Gawain performs poorly due to his weakness and reluctance to be patient. Furthermore, when examining the shortcomings of Sir Gawain mentioned in this article, they can be blamed on the fact that the text originated in France. Unlike the English tales featuring a more heroic and commendable Sir Gawain, French tales did not portray him in such a positive manner.

Sir Gawain's masculinity and other issues of gender are further explored in Edward Kennedy's article "Gawain's Family and Friends: *Sir Gawain and the Green Knight* and Its Allusions to French Prose Romances." One key issue that Kennedy explores is, "...the pentangle that Gawain wears on his shield..." (Kennedy 144). With all that it represents, ranging from integrity to generosity, it is almost safe to conclude that Sir Gawain is a noble and respectable man (Kennedy 144). While it is the stereotypical belief that all men of this era were focused on bloodshed and other violence, Gawain makes it known that he is focused on something deeper. In fact, his dedication towards being pure, compassionate, respectful and honorable set him apart from most other men (Kennedy 144). With the mere presence of Sir Gawain's pentangle decorated shield, he redefines what it means to be both masculine and knightly. Also, there is great importance in where the pentangle is located on Sir Gawain's suit of armor. Being on his shield suggests that Sir Gawain trusts in these values and positive traits enough to protect his life with them. His overwhelming devotion to the pentangle and the values it represents is admirable. Lastly, what it not unusual about this article is that it paints a portrait of a chivalrous and honorable knight. Such an image is nothing new, and only supports the preset definition of what a knight should and should not be. Though, the article does disagree with others as it has Sir Gawain in a positive light.

For *Place, Space, and Landscape in Medieval Narrative*, Sylvia Federico wrote the article "The Place of Chivalry in the New Trojan Court: Gawain, Troilus, and Richard II." Federico strongly goes against what appears to be the norm in stating that Sir Gawain was merely trying to preserve his masculinity (Federico 174). She reinforces this view in explaining that the poem focuses on, "...this threat to masculinity..." (Federico 174). With the Green Knight barging in and making cowards out of the, "...defenders of the realm," it is expected of Sir Gawain to take the masculine route and defend himself from accusations of being weak and cowardly (Federico 174). In fact, the entire journey to find the Green Chapel nearly proves his dedication to defending his reputation. If anything, Sir Gawain was defending far more than just his own reputation, but the reputations of every man who had been insulted at Arthur's court. Federico explains that any failure would, "...further [expose] Arthur's court as a group of foolish children, not fighting men" (Federico 174). Therefore, with these supposedly noble men claiming to be the new rulers of the world, it was critical that their reputations and names remain solid. If they were all proven to be faulty men and halfhearted knights, their reign may fall under question. With that being said, what Sir Gawain set out to accomplish can be seen as nothing short of extraordinary. Not only was he brave in setting out to defend his own honor, he was respectable for in defending the many men of Arthur's court. In sum, according to Federico's article, he is regarded as being a masculine and honorable man.

In the article "Why Dame Ragnell Had to Die: Feminine Usurpation of Masculine Authority in "The Wedding of Sir Gawain and Dame Ragnell" written for *The English 'Loathly Lady' Tales*, Mary Leech explains how Sir Gawain is portrayed outside of *Sir Gawain and the Green Knight*. Instantly, Leech begins her article with, "Gawain as well is unusual in this story" (Leech 213). Leech explains that he is so unusual for not having any obvious flaws (Leech 213). In fact, Leech notes that "Gawain never acts unchivalrously; he is never discourteous to anyone..." (Leech 213). In other words, Sir Gawain appears to be not only the perfect knight, but the perfect man. Leech stresses that this is the case because he is even polite to, "...the hideous Dame Ragnell..." (Leech 213). Stereotypically, men should aim to please only the most beautiful women, and should carry on their duties as knight flawlessly. In short, Sir Gawain even goes far beyond those great expectations. The fact that he is both polite to and marries a hideously ugly woman demonstrates his selfless nature in this tale. Additionally, it has been noted by some that Sir Gawain just barely fell short of perfection in *Sir Gawain and the Green Knight*, but in this story he appears to be what is regarded as perfect. Lastly, his manliness and masculine nature do not suffer in "The Wedding of Sir Gawain and Dame Ragnell" either as he, "...never argues with Arthur, nor does he ever sway from his duty to his king" (Leech 213). He is a true knight's knight, executing all requests perfectly, but also remains admirable in every other way. Moreover, if it is a perfect balance between women and duty that all knights are to aim for, then Sir Gawain has accomplished it in this tale.

In "Courtly Aesthetics and Courtly Ethics in *Sir Gawain and the Green Knight*" written by Jill Mann for *Studies in the Age of Chaucer*, she argues that Sir Gawain performed his deeds for what can be understood as the wrong reasons. In comparison the other articles examined, Mann approaches the tale in a completely different manner. Mann feels as if much of the story is based on the intimidating of, "...the lower classes and maintaining social order by a visible display of wealth and power" (Mann 236). Given that the target audience for *Sir Gawain and the Green Knight* has been gone for quite some time, readers of today's generation sometimes fail to receive the full meaning of the text. Mann does not dispute that Sir Gawain performed the actions listed in the tale, but argues that they were executed for the wrong reasons. One reason was to intimidate the poor who may have heard the story at some point in their lives, and another reason was to help maintain social order. Furthermore, the primary message to be delivered by this text is to not one of good, but one of oppression and control. Any challenger to the upper class will arguably have no effect on the noble subjects. For example, after the ordeal has concluded, Arthur's court moves on nearly undisturbed. In addition, Mann stresses that the celebration of courtly magnificence plays, "...so large a role..." (Mann 241). This could explain how defending the court's honor is so very important. In conclusion, Sir Gawain is seen in a far different light than before after reading Mann's article. He is no longer chivalrous and honorable, but is instead just a tool of the upper class. While his actions are brave and manly, no stereotypically true and honest man could perform such actions for the benefit of oppression and illegitimate control. As a result of Mann's opinionated article, Sir Gawain's masculinity is damaged as he is portrayed as a corrupt person.

In comparing the works, there were many similarities and differences. The articles and their views of Sir Gawain varied not simply due to country of origin, but also due to the lens in which the text was examined. When *Sir Gawain and the Green Knight* is read through a social lens, Sir Gawain appears to be aiding in the oppression of the lower class. Though, the other articles primarily focused on examining his actions and masculinity. Furthermore, it can be concluded that Sir Gawain's image and masculinity largely d epend on the country of origin. In the French tales, Sir Gawain is portrayed as a whiny and intolerable person who focuses on making his complaints known. However, in English tales, he is the complete opposite and nearly achieves perfection. Although masculinity and gender stereotypes in French and English tales were explored to a degree, what remains absent is countries of origin deviating from the norm. In order to fill this gap in research, instances of Sir Gawain being seen in a positive light in France and in a negative light in England must be found. This is key to determining whether strength or weakness primarily dominates Sir Gawain. In conclusion, after conducting research on Sir Gawain's masculinity, it is interesting to see so many unique accounts of just one man.

SOURCES

Federico, Sylvia. "The Place of Chivalry in the New Trojan Court." *Place, Space, and Landscape in Medieval Narrative* (2007): 171-179. Retrieved 2 Apr. 2010.

Gowans, Linda. "Lamenting or Just Grumbling? Arthur's Nephew Expresses His Discontent." *Arthurian Literature* 24 (2007): 91-103. Retrieved 2 Apr. 2010.

Kennedy, Edward. "Gawain's Family and Friends: *Sir Gawain and the Green Knight* and Its Allusions to French Prose Romantics." *People and Texts* (2007): 143-160. Retrieved 2 Apr. 2010.

Lander, Bonnie. "The Convention of Innocence and *Sir Gawain and the Green Knight*'s Literary Sophisticates." *Parergon* 24.1 (2007): 41-66. Retrieved 2 Apr. 2010.

Leech, Mary. "Why Dame Ragnell Had to Die: Feminine Usurpation of Male Authority in 'The Wedding of Sir Gawain and Dame Ragnell.'" *The English 'Loathly Lady' Tales* (2007): 213-234. Retrieved 2 Apr. 2010.

Mann, Jill. "Courtly Aesthetics and Courtly Ethics in *Sir Gawain and the Green Knight*." *Studies in the Age of Chaucer* 31 (2009): 231-265. Retrieved 2 Apr. 2010.

Owen, Corey. "Patient Lancelot and Impatient Gawain in the *Queste del Saint Grael*." *Arthuriana* 17.4 (2007): 3-28. Retrieved 2 Apr. 2010.

Taylor, Jefferey. "Semantic Social Games and the Game of Life in *Sir Gawain and the Green Knight* and *Arrow-Odd's Saga*." *Medieval Forum* (2007): 1-11. Retrieved 2 Apr. 2010.

14. A Glimpse Into the Scholarship Surrounding Entertainment and Realism Within Medieval Drama

The Vulnerability of Man

When the 1994 movie *Pulp Fiction* was released, it was praised for its uniqueness thanks to oddities such as actors stepping out to character to address the audience, its toying with realism and believability, and self-awareness. However, in actuality there is nothing fresh or new about any of these components. In fact, according to scholars, such practices and settings have existed for many hundreds of years. Some medieval plays, for example, have provided their audiences with a believable, realistic experience. Despite the fact that what is believable or realistic varies depending on the audience, many viewers found themselves immersed in plays and in the hands of the actors. Performers were capable of speaking out of character, addressing the audience directly, or even pushing the audience to participate in the production, whether it was mentally or physically. For some, these numerous factors all added up to create what was a gripping and inclusive experience which, at the very least, was a welcomed form of entertainment and introspection for audiences.

On the topic of medieval realism is Alessandro Conti's text "Realism in the Later Middle Ages," which lightly investigates the its presence during the time period. She explains how only recently, when history is considered in its entirety, has the notion of medieval realism come under inspection. Academic journals such as *Vivarium* have grazed the topic, collecting articles and forming collaborative texts in order to pinpoint realism's conception (Conti 2). One such researcher is John Wyclif, an "Oxford Realist" who has partly devoted himself to the topic (2). Conti explains how, "Wyclif is one of the most important and authoritative thinkers of the late Middle Ages and the starting-point of the new forms of realism at the end of the Middle Ages" (3).

While, despite the research of scholars, an actual date has yet to be pinpointed, some theorize that it is in the late medieval period that the modern form of realism came to exist. During the late stages of the Middle Ages, this, "new form of realism [was] inaugurated," and the drastic change in presentation has been noted by select scholars like Conti herself, and other Oxford Realists such as Robert Alyngton and William Milverley (6). However, while scholarship has been done on the topic of an advancing realism, other scholars refute these findings which conflict with their own research.

John Watkins' text "Bedevilling the Histories of Medieval and Early Modern Drama" provides a more critical view of performances during the Middle Ages. He explains how, "even after modernism created an audience for nonrealistic performance, medieval plays still smacked of crudeness and amateurism" (Watkins 69). According to Watkins, not only were said plays simply not realistic, they were only moderately performed. This could be for a number of reasons ranging from the fact that local guilds would perform the plays to the simple lack of serious actors. In the time period between wagon pageants and Shakespearean productions, dramatic performances would experience a meteoric rise in popularity. Meaning that, according to Watkins, the amateurism witnessed on behalf of the medieval actors is not surprising but instead understandable. In addition, the plays may have existed in the same sense that present day horror movies exist for modern viewers. Watkins explains how the plays confronted, "their audiences again and again with the image of a battered, bleeding, killed, buried, and cyclically resurrected savior" (72). This touch of cynicism could be key in determining whether or not the plays pushed for any sense of realism, or they simple aimed to shock or entertain audience members. Given Watkins' supporting evidence taken from the plays themselves, realism does not appear to be obtainable. It is especially not able to be acquired considering the fact that audiences would have been watching Christ of all figures, living out the cycle of his entire life on stage. Furthermore, the presence of this text and its denial of realism and believability raises the question of whether or not audiences

124

may have become immersed in what they were viewing. Additionally, it raises the question of what emotions and reactions may have been present in the audience during the instance of production.

One such instance of crowd reaction is minimally discussed in Maureen Fries' text "The Evolution of Eve in Medieval French and English Religious Drama." In her essay, she brings to light the realism potentially witnessed by medieval audiences during a production by explaining, "in spite of the dignified and devout characters of the York cycle, over which "a fragrance of incense seems to linger," these characters have their realistic and even lively moments, such as the quarrel of the two first people in the Armourers' Play" (Fries 11). Her investigation into crowd emotions in reaction to the play provides for two interesting perspectives: first, that the York cycle was far less realistic, and that this was due to the fact that the characters were calm and "dignified"; second, that liveliness correlates with realness. If Fries examination of crowd reactions is to be believed, the more rugged, lively, and wild plays may have been regarded by audiences as more realistic, thus providing for a far higher entertainment value. On the contrary, Fries' research is not without challengers of its own.

In "Power and Conflict in Medieval Ritual Plays: The Re-Invention of Drama," Norma Kroll's research into audience-actor relations provides for a conflicting description of "dignified" productions. While Fries may have previously explained how lively productions were "realistic," it is noted by Kroll that religious plays could indeed achieve the same result from the audience. She explains, "cleric-playwrights and their worshipper-audiences found truth in their metaphoric interpretations of earthly (and cosmic) reality, while recognizing that metaphors are not to be read factually" (Kroll 467). Her research attempts to show how religious plays performed two interesting functions: they provided the audiences with a sense of truth, despite the fact that they were more calmly and carefully presented, and they achieved truth without fact. Meaning that, according to her research, audiences could view the religiously themed plays in question and gain knowledge and a resulting higher sense of understanding, all without having the plays be wild and enthusiastic, or even believable. The mild presentation of metaphors and alone was enough to have certain audiences hooked, resulting in focused and decidedly involved onlookers. Additionally, what is most striking about select religious plays was their ability to become both creative and abstract in their presentations, all the while still having a grip on their audiences. Kroll points out how, "the playwrights [would] join imaginative fictions [and] ritual reality" (483). This practice would allow playwrights to flex their imaginations and provide audiences with their own takes on religious events which were set in stone. Moreover, for some audience members, the events on stage seemed to be a, "real re-creation of Christ's presence and actions" (453). Kroll attributes this created realness to the power of creativity. She further explains how, "tenth-century inventiveness led to other ceremonies that, like the Eucharistic rite, allowed Christ to manifest his real presence" (465). If Kroll's examination of crowd reaction is to provide concrete evidence of anything, it is the reality that realism is in the hands of the audience. While some crowds strongly preferred a passionate and chaotic delivery, others bought into moderate presentations of religious imaginativeness. Others, however, may not have bought into anything at all, no matter what the style of presentation or the topic at hand. Another subtopic which may provide some insight into realism, believability and the entertainment factor is audience interaction.

A key factor in determining the relationship between a play and its audience is the interaction of the two. Venturing back to John Watkins' "Bedevilling the Histories of Medieval and Early Modern Drama," he provides for some insight as to how crowds may have reacted to select plays. Initially, he expresses the difficulty in pinpointing the, "the ability of early audiences to tolerate inherent ambiguities in theatrical illusion" (Watkins 75). With the possible presence of unclear meanings, Watkins stresses that audiences may not have appreciated the reality of not knowing exactly what the play was talking about. Such reactions from audiences even persists today, with movies host to unclear narratives and morals subject to ridicule and criticism. To expand upon this, another instance of crowd interaction comes with the practice of audience participation.

According to medieval scholars, with Maureen Fries' text "The Evolution of Eve in Medieval French and English Religious Drama" included, the audience would often participate in the production of the play. She notes that, in one scene, "the devil tells [Adam] to think it over, and he and his demons take a turn around the audience; but Adam is adamant in his virtue" (Fries 3). Whether it wants to or not, the audience, at the direction of the devil, is part of his games and ensuing pandemonium. Such an instance of participation from the audience points out the important existence, or arguable lack of existence, of the "fourth wall" in drama. Jeanne McCarthy explores this issue in her text ""The Sanctuarie is become a plaiers stage": Chapel Stagings and Tudor "Secular" Drama." She explains how certain characters even go out of their way in order to break down the fourth wall, or the theoretical wall in between the stage and the audience; the wall that, when broken, joins actor and audience together as one. She states that one character, "dismisses the players and audience" (McCarthy 69). This action appears to be meant to exclude the audience from the play, but actually creatively acknowledges their existence. Moreover, some stage directions even directed the audience as to where to go during the conclusion of the play. These lines, "of the play are used as a prompt for the dishbearers to lead the audience into the adjacent banqueting hall for the meal" (69). Having characters speak directly to the audience and control their next moves immerses the audience. Another example of a play's concluding lines interacting with the audience is noted by McCarthy, "Perseverance's final lines in which he prays that the audience too might be brought "unto Vertuous living" and the "bliss of heaven... Amen"" (76). What McCarthy provides is an example of introspection, or spiritual self examination of the audience. Also, some actors even asked for the opinions of the audience, by inviting, "the audience's admiration" (77). Lastly, what is the most unusual example of crowd participation is the asking of audience members to use their imaginations. For example, McCarthy explains, "the iconic scene of Our Lady of Pity in which [a character] asks the audience to contemplate a virtual character onstage" (75). Having a medieval audience create a character from their own imagination not only allows for a deeper sense of involvement on behalf of the crowd, but also allows for viewers to flex their own imaginations. While this level of immersion may not necessarily be realistic or believable, it served a different purpose: it brought the audience into a realm which it shared with the actors. If anything, it provided for a higher level of entertainment, because it encouraged an active audience. Despite examining the scholarship surrounding audience participation and involvement, as well as medieval realism and believability, what is left out is the study of a crucial factor that may have a large influence on the audience: gender.

In his text titled "*Dux Moraud*: Criminality and Salvation in an East Anglican Play," Clifford Davidson explores the presence of male authority in medieval drama. He notes that many lines, "contain the male speaker's command for attention from the audience and his assertion of authority" (Davidson 128). It is important to take note that a male actor would not ask for, but demand attention from his audience. Davidson expands upon this fact, explaining, "in production he surely would have projected a commanding appearance and one that appropriately reflected his self-love, a form of love that seems to reach out to embrace the audience" (129). While he did not say that it did reach out to the audience, Davidson notices how it "seems to," and for some reason this self-love was appealing to medieval audiences. The male's strong, commanding tone would conjure up a rise in attention from onlookers. However, just as easily as male characters could grip an audience, they would also be expected to make themselves vulnerable, and open themselves up to their viewers. Davidson explains how some male actors would confess their issues to the audience, in an open manner which begged for judgment and reaction from the audience (132). It is in Davidson's research that the issue of gender finally takes a front seat and is one of the main focuses. Even though female characters were in existence, it was often male participants who were expected to involve, dismiss, grip or even confess their sins to the audience.

Entertainment is comprised of varying components: believability and realism, audience interaction and potential participation, and even the oddity of character self-awareness. While some may believe these traits to be postmodern, a review of scholarship focusing on medieval drama shows that they are not. In fact, they are quite old. For hundreds of years, proof has existed that audiences would become a part of the production, and that they would be entertained in creative manners. Whether this was done by a having a play flood out through the fourth wall and into the audience, or through characters pushing viewers to look inward at themselves, what resulted was an oftentimes powerful experience. Medieval productions were capable of not just entertaining, but allowing audiences to think deeply, become immersed and be directed with tactics that were by some suspected of maturing in the postmodern era.

SOURCES

Conti, Alessandro. "Realism in the Later Middle Ages." *Vivarium* 43:1 (2005): 1-6. *MLA Bibliography.* Web. 1 Nov. 2011.

Davidson, Clifford. "*Dux Moraud*: Criminality and Salvation in an East Anglican Play." *Medieval & Renaissance Drama in England* 22 (2009): 128-143. *MLA Bibliography.* Web. 1 Nov. 2011.

Fries, Maureen. "The Evolution of Eve in Medieval French and English Religious Drama." *Studies in Philology* 99:1 (2002): 1-16. *MLA Bibliography.* Web. 1 Nov. 2011.

Kroll, Norma. "Power and Conflict in Medieval Ritual and Plays: The Re-Invention of Drama." North Carolina: The University of North Carolina Press, 2005. 452-483. *MLA Bibliography.* Web. 1 Nov. 2011.

McCarthy, Jeanne. ""The Sancuarie is become a plaiers stage": Chapel Stagings and Tudor "Secular" Drama." *Medieval & Renaissance Drama in England* (2008): 56-86. *MLA Bibliography.* Web. 1 Nov. 2011.

Watkins, John. "Bedevilling the Histories of Medieval and Early Modern Drama." Illinois: The University of Chicago, 2003. 68-78. Web.

15. John Donne's Bold New Cosmological Model in "The Sun Rising"

Man as Bold

The English language is particularly fluid. It is in a state of continuous change and evolution that is sometimes noticed within the span of a few years or decades, but is easily noticed when examining definitions established centuries prior. Despite authorial intention, what is said now may not be what is said after a great deal of time passes. Depending on the reader, this fact could be the case for John Donne's "The Sun Rising" as the lines could be misinterpreted. The lines in question are the final two, where John Donne's speaker states that his bedroom is the center of the universe and that the sun revolves around them both. Today's contemporary audience may mistake the lines for stating that their lovemaking is merely important to Donne's speaker, but a much deeper meaning is to be uncovered through historical research. According to researchers such as Edward Rosen and Stanley Aronowitz, the church was absolutely against any who would suggest that the center of the universe was anything but the earth. Also, Karen Bennett and Maurice A. Finocchiaro explore the life of Galileo and further explain how the church would have never accepted the cosmological model proposed by Donne's speaker. With the long lasting sensitivity within the church surrounding the issue of heliocentrism, the speaker's new layout for the universe with his bedroom resting at the center, whether stated jokingly or seriously, is risky as it could have resulted in a damaged reputation or even worse.

In John Donne's "The Sun Rising," the speaker focuses on his lovemaking with a beautiful woman, its importance, and downplaying the importance of the nobility, religious beliefs and scientific theories. Above all else rests his lovemaking, and everything else pales in comparison. While he does insult education and the nobility, the most crucial lines of the poem are final two in which he states, "Shine here to us, and thou art everywhere; This bed thy center is, these walls thy sphere" (Donne 29-30). The two lines in question may first appear to be insignificant as he is merely suggesting that she is his focus while they are in the act of lovemaking, but the lines would hold much more meaning when initially penned by Donne. To better locate the meaning of the lines, historical context comes into play as it allows for readers to understand exactly what is being said by Donne's speaker. By performing focused historical research, Donne's final lines are illuminated with meaning that may have slipped by contemporary readers. Given the lines' topic of cosmology and the center of the universe, focused research of scientific studies conducted just prior to and during the life of Donne is essential. Specifically, the two primary figures of the research will be Copernicus for his proposal of heliocentrism, and Galileo for his eventual defense of the theory in the Roman courts. In doing so, the severity of the speaker's statements will be established, and contemporary readers will be able to read the final two lines of "The Sun Rising" with a full understanding of what it is Donne's speaker was attempting to say. Furthermore, researching the past will help to determine whether or not proposing a new cosmological model, whether jokingly or not, is a bold or even extreme move on behalf of Donne. With that being said, researching Copernicus' stunning publication *Revolutions* is the best place to start as it is the moment where the controversial topic began.

Before venturing into the life of Copernicus, a brief yet crucial visit must be paid to the history of science in general during the time period. To put the newness of modern science into perspective, it must be noted that common practices such as modern dentistry had not even begun as of this time. This advancement would not occur until the seventeenth century, when Pierre Fauchard begins to make great strides in dentistry. Until this time, what we now know as science consisted of unproven remedies and spiritual healing. In addition, science rarely had the chance to greatly conflict with religious beliefs. With that being said, it becomes more clear as to why heliocentrism deeply offended the church. For once, a scientific theory

131

directly stated that the competing religious theory must be false. In stating that a theory of religion must be false, a controversy was ignited by Copernicus.

In order to better understand John Donne's "The Sun Rising," it is important to investigate key scientific findings of the time period. While Copernicus himself had been dead for a few decades before John Donne's writing began, what survives are his ideas. At first glance, what seem as if they are the mere theories of an astronomer would actually come to cause controversy within the world of western religion. Particularly angering the Catholics, Copernicus suggested his studies prove that the age old belief in the Ptolemaic model of the solar system was false. Rather, he stated it was the sun that stayed in place as the planets revolved around it in a somewhat predictable manner. With religion's stranglehold on Europe, this conflicting discovery created a controversy as it would dare to challenge the established view of the solar system. In this case, giving a yard could result in a mile's worth of distance by the time the debate was settled. Meaning, if religion could ever be proven wrong once, perhaps science could disprove its theories once more. Also, the theories and established ideas disproved could gain in strength, further lessening the strength of Christianity. This destructive pattern is what Copernicus' model set in motion, and his ideas would soon become a serious nuisance for the church.

Edward Rosen's "Was Copernicus' *Revolutions* Approved by the Pope?" further sheds light on these conflicting ideas and their reception within the religious world. According to him, the rise of science contributes to the rise in popularity for people similar to Copernicus. He states, "as the humanist attitude spread, lay contributors to culture became more influential than had been when clerics were dominant" (Rosen 531). In other words, many contributors to math and science suddenly found themselves in the spotlight, or at least much more than before the rise of science, instead of members of religion. It is important to remember that Copernicus taught in a post-Mongol invasion return of Greek philosophy. The culture in which he lived was alive with a newfound love for science and mathematics. However, with one's rise came another's fall, and religion seemed to be less of a focus for members of society. The prominence of science would cause turmoil in the religious world, but Rosen ponders the actual reception of Copernicus' ideas by the Catholic church.

Rosen explores the idea that the Catholic church may have been much less fearful of Copernicus' ideas than previously thought. For example, he makes note of there being numerous, "humanistically productive monks and friars" (531). In addition, he explains how, "at the time of the Fifth Lateran Council (1517-17), the pope appealed to the experts for suggestions about improving the calendar, which was known to be out of phase with the seasons" (531). In other words, the church was receptive of select scientific ideas, and Copernicus actually felt comfortable with contacting them. Rosen explains that "Many specialists replied, including Nicholas Copernicus, whose response has not been found" (531). This fact is interesting, because it deletes the idea that Copernicus cowered in fear of the Catholic church, as if they absolutely hated him and the ideas he developed. While his ideas were radical and controversial, creating anger in some religious members, he was never hated to a degree that threatened bodily harm. Continuing with the explanation, Rosen states that "after the Fifth Lateran Council ended in 1517 without reaching a definite decision about reforming the calendar, further researchers were encouraged by the papacy" (532). This statement is important, because it shows that these requests for researchers were not made by random, minimally powerful members of the church, but actually the pope himself. The leader of the Catholic church supported the ideas which were later deemed unbearably controversial.

Even though the initial stance of the pope appears to be favorable, it is lesser known that much of his particularly extreme favoritism was actually fake. Rosen explains that Copernicus' first biographer completely made up the story of undeniable favoritism, yet the fairytale has lasted with researchers for some time. The first biography of Copernicus was written by, "the famous polymath Bernardino Baldi (1553-1617)" (534). Rosen then explains, "Baldi had before him the letter sent to Copernicus by Nicholas Schonberg, cardinal of Capua, on 1 November 1536" (534). He then states that, in the letter, it was written, "Schonberg had Copernicus' work; recognized its perfection and excellence; showed it to the pope, by whose judgment it was approved" (534). While this fact may seem to be a dream come true for Copernicus, there is the unfortunate fact that what was written is not the truth. Astonishingly, Baldi filled his first biography of Copernicus with mild to major fabrications. Of course, the lie told about Schonberge's approval of the Copernican model was the worst, because it attempted to change history. In reality, the pope was indeed searching for scientists to help perfect the Catholic calendar, but he in no way favored Copernicus' ideas to such an extent.

What really happened is much less spectacular as it was confined by the limited technology of the age. According to Rosen, Schonberg could have never read Copernicus' work, because he died after suffering from ill health on 9 September 1537, a little more than 10 months after the letter is dated. Rosen explains that "This interval … was hardly long enough to encompass travel from Rome to Poland and back again, with the copying of the *Revolutions* sandwiched in between the two trips" (534). Rosen means that, in taking the slowness of travel into account along with the extremely slow process of copying and printing, there is no possible way that Schonberg could have read and approved of Copernicus' *Revolutions*. At the very best, the cardinal was intrigued, but he was not at all in favor of his work. Therefore, according to Rosen, it is clear that "Schonberg did not have the *Revolutions* before he wrote to Copernicus on 1 November 1536" (534). He further explains that, as a result of uncovering the truth, "the rest of Baldi's contrived scenario disappears" (534). Within an instant, his idea, "vanished in thin air" (534). Rosen's further exploration of Baldi's work shows that the church was absolutely not in favor of Copernicus' work.

The historical inaccuracy of Baldi's first publication is troubling as it suggests that the church was in full support of the Copernican model, when in actuality it was not. It becomes clear that the biographer knew much less than what he initially suggested as he later states, "I would not know," about Copernicus' reward for *Revolutions*' approval (534-535). Such a misstep is only topped by the fact that he also mistook the actions of pope Paul III with his immediate predecessor Clement VII (535). Definitively, researchers know there is no hint of Copernicus ever mentioning a papal order, approval, or permission (536). Rosen then states, "these pronouncements by Baldi ... were issued far from Rome some four to eight decades after the (pretended) event" (536). In conclusion, despite the mild skepticism surrounding the pope's stance on *Revolutions*, it is definitely not the case that the pope was in full support of Copernicus' publication. In fact, his findings were shown interest but were ultimately found to be insulting and offensive to the church. Despite Rosen's research, perhaps one other writer's findings can help to pinpoint the boldness of heliocentrism.

In Stanley Aronowitz's "The Politics of the Science Wars," he takes to the issue of heliocentrism which appears to rest neatly in between positive and negative, and attempts to better define it. He writes that Copernicus' theory helped, "explain a broad range of phenomena," and it, "showed that Ptolemaic cosmology was not radically different from that of Copernicus" (Aronowitz 192). In other words, when examined, both models of the solar system are not really so different. Both generally follow the same guidelines with one solar object orbiting another. Perhaps the speaker's statement that it is he who rests in the center of the universe is not too radical at all. However, on the other hand, some critics felt that in defending the Copernican theory, "Galileo's "proof" that the earth was in constant motion around the sun, and Newtonian mechanics were not "superior" to Ptolemaic science" (191). These opposing views mean that Donne's writing could be either highly offensive or not that offensive at all. If Rosen and Aronowitz's findings are not convincing enough, it is crucial to turn to the life of Galileo, a strong defender of the Copernican model who lived during the time period in which John Donne was writing.

Arriving at Galileo, there is perhaps no better historical figure to help the reader better understand the boldness of Donne's language. In "The Sun Rising," it is important to turn to Karen Bennett's "Galileo's Revenge: Ways of Construing Knowledge and Translation Strategies in the Era of Globalization." Long after he had passed away, Copernicus' ideas continued onward, mainly with Galileo's, "confrontation with the Catholic Church in 1616 over Copernicanism, the injunction issued against him, and his eventual trial and disgrace in 1633" (Bennett 171). If there was any doubt on whether or not the ideas presented by Copernicus a generation prior were offending, Bennett's article helps to end any remaining debate. In fact, Bennett goes as far as to say that "the event is usually portrayed as the first major conflict in a long war between religion and science, in which the latter was to emerge as inevitably victorious" (171). This statement shows how, once Copernicus had passed away, his ideas still remained strong and menacing for the church. Additionally, Bennett explains that "until around the time of Galileo's fateful confrontation with the Holy Office, an entirely different theory of knowledge was dominant in England, as in the rest of Europe" (174). In other words, when Donne's speaker makes the possibly sarcastic yet profound statement that his lovemaking rests in the center of the universe, it goes against not only what was the dominant cosmological belief in England, but in most of Europe as well. As for Galileo, his confrontation with the church was more widely recognized, because it was a, "gradual removal of a veil of misrepresentation about the natural world that had for centuries been held in place by the interests of the Church" (171). In short, given the sensitive nature of Copernicus' ideas and Galileo's defense, the statements made by the speaker in rejection of the dominant cosmological belief were as daring as they were shocking.

Further exploring the life of Galileo and his conflict with religion helps readers to better understand the severity of John Donne's writings. With Donne and Galileo living during the same time period, and sensitivity still

136

lingering alongside heliocentrism, the daring nature of the speaker's words is better understood. Maurice A. Finocchiaro's text "The Church and Galileo" helps readers to understand the enduring sensitivity surrounding the Copernican model and those in support of the theory. He explains that, later in time, "Galileo's elaborated views about scriptural interpretation and its relationship to scientific and philosophical investigation that were later implicitly accepted by Pope Leo XIII" (Finocchiaro 262). However, even though the first event appears to be a totally positive, it is crucial to understand that this move did not happen until 1893. In addition, this acceptance of Galileo's views was mild at best as his views were not totally accepted until the reign of Pope John Paul II in 1979. Finocchiaro explains that it was only able to take place during the centennial of Einstein's birth, and that "Pope John Paul II gave a speech in which he talked about the Galileo affair" (275). This full-on acceptance would happen many hundreds of years after the lives of Copernicus, Galileo and Donne, and it serves to show the enduring sensitivity of the issue. For Donne to have even joking wrote, "Shine here to us, and thou art everywhere; This bed thy center is, these walls thy sphere" was nothing short of risky, and well within the realm of dangerous (Donne 29-30). While the danger may not be strictly physical, it certainly could affect his job within the church or his overall reputation. Finocchiaro ventures further into the issue of redefining the cosmos in order to make the issue of Galileo and Copernicus all the more clear.

According to Finocchiaro, Pope Urban VIII was anti-astrological, and was reigning in 1631 (266). While 1631 is the year of Donne's death and within a decade of Galileo's, what was lingering strong were the ideas. The offensiveness of the theories was as strong as ever during this time period. Moving onward, as for the events surrounding Copernicus specifically, Finocchiaro states that "This condemnation was the climax of a series of events that started in 1543, when Nicolaus Copernicus published an epoch-making book, *On the Revolutions of the Heavenly Spheres*" (261). It is noted that this moment is the one, "in which he advanced a new argument in favor of the idea that the earth revolves around the sun" (261). Finocchiaro writes that the new theory, "immediately came under attack for reasons stemming from astronomical observation" (261). In other words, unlike previously suggested in sources above, there was absolutely no acceptance of these radical ideas, and there was immediate hatred shown towards Copernicus. Moreover, along with Copernicus, the speaker's statements of debatable sincerity would have even angered supporters of Aristotelian physics and cosmology. Lastly, Finocchiaro ends his text with another shocking fact: according to him, not even Galileo was a supporter at first, but changed his mind after a staggering twenty years (261). Copernicus' ideas were initially even far too radical for Galileo, one of his most faithful and notable supporters. The fact that it took Galileo two decades to believe in heliocentrism illustrates its bold nature. To reiterate, for Donne to daringly write that the speaker's bedroom, or specifically his bed, was the center of the universe in which the sun revolved was a move to be remembered.

The speaker's statement of his bedroom being the new center of the universe is bold as the sensitive topic of heliocentrism still lingered in the world of Christianity. While modern audiences may not understand the importance of his statements, audiences reading his controversial lines hundreds of years ago may have. According to Karen Bennett and Maurice A. Finocchiaro, the supportive Galileo was still defending the Copernican model of the solar system during the lifetime of Donne, and that helps to prove that heliocentrism was still a hot topic. In fact, heliocentrism has been a sore subject since its proposal, and, according to both Edward Rosen and Stanley Aronowitz, it was never once fully supported by the church until the late twentieth century. With this historical research, modern readers are able to better understand the world in which Donne was writing, and what topics were on the minds of sixteenth and seventeenth century citizens. Admittedly, it is difficult to understand the meaning of a poem when its language is English. Always subject to shifts both mild and major, drastic changes and gradual evolution, the English language is much more fluid than it is solid.

This fact is why it is important to establish historical context. In doing so, modern readers are provided with a better opportunity to definitively understand the poem, its choice of words, and how current events in the time of its writing may be more influential than previously thought.

SOURCES

Aronowitz, Stanley. "The Politics of the Science Wars." *Social Text* 46 (1996): 177-197. *JSTOR*. Web. 2 Feb. 2011.

Bennett, Karen. "Galileo's Revenge: Ways of Construing Knowledge and Translation Strategies in the Era of Globalization." *Social Semiotics* 17:2 (2007): 171-193. *JSTOR*. Web. 2 Feb. 2011.

Donne, John. "The Sun Rising." *Luminarium: Anthology of English Literature*. Accessed 14 Feb. 2011.

Finocchiaro, Maurice. *The Church and Galileo*. Ed. Ernan McMullin. Indiana: University of Notre Dame Press, 2005. 260-282. Web.

Rosen, Edward. "Was Copernicus' *Revolutions* Approved by the Pope?" *Journal of the History of Ideas* 36.2 (1975): 531-542. *JSTOR*. Web. 2 Feb. 2011.

16. Looking Deeper Into Issues Within Wordsworth's "The world is too much with us"

Man, the Caretaker

It is not uncommon to see problems in the past remaining equally as problematic in the present. For example, many readers can still relate to Shakespeare and Chaucer due to their commentary on marriage and relationships. Many issues are seemingly timeless. One such problem that should not be timeless is the pollution of the earth's environment. The issue rose in popularity in the early days of heavy machinery and mass production, and remains unsolved today. One poet who discusses how damaging humans are to the planet is William Wordsworth with his sonnet "The world is too much with us." The poem is important for two reasons: people can still relate to the problems it addresses, and it sheds light on the fact that pollution has not changed for the better in centuries. Though humans have had hundreds of years to use their powers to improve the earth's condition and correct their erroneous ways, nothing has improved and pollution remains worse than ever before.

The condition of life has not improved since 1807, when William Wordsworth wrote "The world is too much with us." He believed that life is all about nature, and human beings' relationship with it. If nature is disrespected and treated poorly, then the condition of life is lowered considerably. However, if people learn to cherish nature, life will eventually improve. In 1807, technology was improving and rendering work more efficient. With these technological advancements, however, came vast amounts of pollution. Wordsworth and other similar poets noticed this destruction, and voiced their opinions on the crucial matter. Since then, nothing has changed for the better, and the pollution has increased at an exponential rate. Alongside this exponential growth comes a worsening quality of living. In present day, we have terrible lives due to our disrespect of nature. In short, humans fail to limit their detrimental effects on the earth. Therefore, it is from human beings' unchanging disrespect for the earth that this sonnet gains its importance. The same issues Wordsworth faced over two centuries ago still remain alive and well today. They have yet to be fixed, and have only become worse.

In William Wordsworth's sonnet, it is explained that humans are harmful to the world. In the first line of the poem, he writes, "The world is too much with us; late and soon" (Wordsworth 1). The world is imperfect with human beings inhabiting it. This conclusion on the state of our planet comes from the fact that humans serve to destroy, ruin and damage everything in nature. Also, no matter what the time in history, we are still far too much for the planet to handle. When looking to the past, it is not difficult to conjure up thoughts of extreme pollution and destruction. Everything from the multiple decades of nuclear testing to the fact that the streets of London were once covered with human and animal waste points to this conclusion of humans being a detrimental presence. Moreover, that very same conclusion can be applied to the present. Humans continue to pollute the environment, and do little to limit or end it.

One issue that continues today is our inability to make good use of our powers. In line two, Wordsworth states, "Getting and spending, we lay waste our powers" (Wordsworth 2). Humans have the power to limit the amount of pollution, yet most choose to ignore it. While people may not have always had the resources we have today, the potential to stop pollution remains unchanged. Furthermore, Wordsworth would most likely be distraught if he were alive today and could see the pollution. Surely, there were great amounts of pollution during his time period, and its effects were quite harmful. However, when pollution is examined in its current state it is easy to see that the problems have been amplified. For example, the rain forests, a major source of the world's oxygen, are being destroyed at an increasing rate. Machines have become all too efficient in mowing down trees and other forms of vegetation. In addition, the oceans are also facing extreme amounts of pollution. Between the dumping of harmful chemicals such as toxic waste, or overfishing, the oceans of the world are in grave danger. "The world is too much with us" was published in 1807, and it is apparent that nothing has improved significantly in these last two centuries.

Another problem existing within the issue of global pollution is the disrespect shown to a higher power. With so many people believing in a supreme being who created the planet, it is a wonder pollution even exists. Assuming that a God created the earth and all of the elements of nature, it is unbelievable that so many could continue damaging it. For poets such as Wordsworth, God created nature, and is nature itself. Destroying nature is outright offending the creator, and such a practice is absurd. Additionally, humans have had far too much influence over nature in the past, and have even more today. One example of this is our ability to construct and maintain cities such as Las Vegas, Nevada in arid, dry, and usually uninhabitable deserts. Simply put, such an idea is not natural and is going against God. Wordsworth supports this idea with, "Little we see in Nature that is ours" (Wordsworth 3). In other words, nature is not ours to manipulate and change. Nature is a product of God, and is not for humans to enforce our destructive ways upon.

Similar to today, when Wordsworth wrote this sonnet many humans were altering nature. The presence of humans and our destructive ways have been made known throughout the world, and in every environment. Our presence affects not just the oceans and the land, but the winds as well (Wordsworth 5-7). The damage extends far into the atmosphere, and it is not natural for the earth to be this way. Wordsworth exclaims that "For this, for every thing, we are out of tune" (Wordsworth 8). Due to our inability to protect the lands, seas and air, and for all other injustices, we are not in sync with the planet. For example, before humanity, the earth carried on to its own cycle. It has a very distinct method of death and regeneration. Once humans began rising to power, however, nothing has been in synchronization. In both 1807 and the present, the earth is an increasingly inefficient machine. Its well established and concrete cycle have been offset by our harmful practices, and it is up to humans to set it right again.

In light of our harm to the planet, many people have turned to paganism and other forms of nature-based religion. It is not uncommon to see people who believe that nature itself is either God, or the product of a higher power. Many people believe that anything man made, even religions such as Christianity, is both temporary and unnatural. Even today, with all of the massive technological leaps, nothing is permanent. No man made thing lasts forever, and it is only nature that stands the test of time. While the pyramids erode, steel rusts and computers falter, nature carries on in a constant state of regeneration and rebirth. Furthermore, it is believed that nature holds the key to divinity as its cycle of regeneration is infinite and everlasting. Wordsworth similarly states that "...I'd rather be / A Pagan suckled in a creed outworn" (Wordsworth 9-10). Though the religion has mostly died out, he would rather be associated with the divinity found in nature than anything else. Furthermore, similar issues exist today as some people have turned towards nature for spiritual needs and inspiration.

Since 1807, methods to limit and reduce the pollution of the earth have been far outnumbered by new and more efficient methods of destruction. The problem of humans remaining static over the issue is rendered all the worse by the fact that we have the power and ability to change the world for the better. In addition, though much of the world believes in some sort of creator who produced the earth, many people continue to contribute substantially to these detrimental effects. As long as the problems of human-led destruction and planetary disrespect persist, the earth will forever be out of sync, and plagued by an unnatural presence.

SOURCE

Wordsworth, William. "The world is too much with us." *The Norton Anthology of English Literature*. Ed. Stephen Greenblatt. New York: W. W. Norton & Company, 2006. 1550.

17. Slavery and Revolution in Blake's *America: a Prophecy* and American History

Man as Visionary

Many issues that existed in earlier times persist today, providing for a relationship between the past and present. One such issue is slavery, in all its forms. Existing in the period of time in which Blake wrote, slavery was a hot topic as an interest in abolitionism was continuing to rise. Faced with trying times and difficult issues, Blake took notice of the world around him and took interest in slavery and liberation through revolution. In an event that would have undoubtedly interest him, Blake observed the events surrounding the American revolution. In addition to witnessing the crucial present conflict and interpreting the recent past, Blake set his focus to the future and wrote *America: a Prophecy* in 1793. His prophecy, or prediction of the future, discusses numerous events. However, given his personal interest in abolitionism and slavery, it is no wonder that one of the focuses of the text was the liberation of others. This focus raises the question: what would Blake think of America's history and its current events in regards to enslavement? It is possible that he would look at various elements of society and be displeased, yet examine other current events and be pleased with what he found. In fact, if Blake had knowledge of America's history and its recent current events, he would most likely criticize the society for reasons such as economic slavery and the treatment of the lower classes, but also approve of our willingness to liberate select countries through the use of brute force.

While it may not be blatantly present in his writings, Blake is thought to have been enveloped by the events surrounding revolutions both in America and elsewhere. In her essay "William Blake and America: Freedom and Violence in the Atlantic World," Clare Elliott expands upon this idea in stating, "the

American interest in Blake's poetry is complemented by his fascination with the events in the Atlantic World in the years culminating in the American War of Independence" (Elliott 209). For Blake, the Revolutionary War was less about sheer chaos and pandemonium and more about freedom and liberation. Elliott states how Blake's poetry, "was particularly suited to the nineteenth-century American psyche" (211). Of course, the central focus of the 1800s being the American Civil War, or a time when the South fought for their own freedom and the North fought for the freedom of the slave population. Expanding her argument, Elliott feels as if Blake's poetry, "would have excited the American imagination in the nineteenth century, as the leading writers and thinkers of the day attempted to understand their dual position in a country which had severed ties with its colonial rule less than a century earlier" (211). Meaning that, with America having a slave population of its own, many citizens began to remember their own pasts which included being dominated by another country. With that being said, it is no wonder that Blake was aware, "of the real iron chains imprisoning countless Africans" (215). Slavery and revolution, or a liberation from outside rule and domination, go hand in hand, and America was at the center of a crossroads between the two. Blake could not help but show great interest in the newly formed country and its predicament.

In regards to his writings, Blake may have regarded revolution as an instance of imaginative freedom. According to Elliott, "Blake's *America* is his effort to exhibit, at once, his ardent support of revolution" (212). His support for revolution and liberation are centered around the character named, "Orc, who is at once the spirit of freedom inspiring the American revolt and as such he is inherently violent" (212). The violence witnessed at the hands of Orc may first appear to be excessive or unnecessary, but given that it is used for the freedom from occupation, it is for the better. Elliott states, "Blake's *America* takes this a stage further by suggesting that even *imaginative* revolution implies violence" (213). The reader is supposed to witness the actions in the poem and cheer him and his, "imaginative capacity," even if it includes violence (213). For Blake, revolution was not a time of much hated mystery, but was instead a clean palette, or the chance for pure imagination to flourish.

Briefly touching on the Civil War in America, an interesting dilemma arises out of a paradoxical situation. With Blake's love for freedom and revolution, and his hatred for slavery, it is difficult to predict his stance on the Civil War. His prediction of the enslaved becoming freed in *America: a Prophecy* would most likely rest at being half true (Blake 43). This problem exists because, no matter what the outcome of the Civil War, a group of people were not allowed to free themselves. For example, if the Confederacy were to have won the war, they would have achieved freedom thanks to their revolution. No matter if it came as a result of violent battles and bitter disputes, the revolt would be a success. However, on the other hand, the Confederacy was dedicated to keeping slaves due to racial beliefs and financial reasons. If they had won the war, slaves would still remain being used and exploited. It seems as if there is no right or wrong side to choose, assuming Blake's opinions are applied to the situation. Yet, if choosing a side were a must, Blake would have most likely been swept up by the wave of abolitionism taking over America. While the Confederacy was certainly fighting for their version of freedom, not all freedoms are created equal. With African, Caribbean and Asian slavery being considered, Blake may have supported the liberation of African American slaves within the South. Their actual iron manacles and the desire to be free from them would gain more support than the freedom to use such tools and control others. The revolution and fight for the liberation of the Confederacy would have no doubt interested Blake, but it is more likely that this interest would pale in comparison to his devotion to the freeing of African American slaves.

Whether it is social conventions that bind a person or actual iron manacles, anything that withholds both creative and physical freedom is an enemy of William Blake. In Christine Gallant's "Blake's Antislavery Designs for *Songs of Innocence and of Experience*," she explores slavery in relation to Blake's poetry and American society. Blake wrote a few prophecies, or predictions of the future, but none dealt more explicitly with physical slavery than *America: A Prophecy*. Gallant explains how, "Blake's prophecies may allude to slave revolts with the burning cane fields" (Gallant 123). With European societies having witnessed a number of revolts both minor and major, some citizens were well aware of slavery's potentially violent outcomes. Having mentioned his concept of "mind forg'd manacles" before, William Blake was no stranger to both the physical and mental horrors of slavery.

In regards to physical slavery, Blake had the mindset of an 18th century abolitionist. Gallant notes how, "William Blake may not have been part of the 18th century Black Atlantic but he was often close to its perspective" (Gallant 123). While Blake may not have taken part in the infamous Atlantic slave trade, citizens of Britain were no strangers to the concept of slavery and the violence by which it was surrounded. According to Gallant, he would have been mindful of sugar plantations, as well as other slavery in West India (130). On the mainland, British citizens were often critical of slavery and had been among the first to push for abolition. Gallant states that "several years before 1789, when Blake composed the *Songs of Innocence*, British abolitionism had become a widespread movement" (123). However, the British empire's reach extended far beyond the handful of islands resting above Europe. By this time, solid trade routes had been established and the British as well as Europeans were being introduced to new, exotic and addicting substances. With said addiction came excitement, and in a manner similar to today's consumerism, excitement resulted in both demand profit. However, this profit was nothing minor, but was instead astonishing. In fact, suppliers could barely keep up with purchaser's demands, and the resulting heightened amount of trade relied on hard labor, slavery and especially exploitation. Whether or not Blake would enjoy this fact, most everyone on the British mainland either directly or indirectly took part in slavery. Additionally, slave issues and revolts found their way into

Blake's mind. Gallant explains how, "the antislavery movement and its concomitant slave revolts, especially of Saint-Domingue, inspired his poetry and designs" (123). While some of Blake's works did not mention slavery in a straightforward manner, the presence of slavery is still identifiable. It is stated, "although the texts may not seem to relate to abolitionist concerns or slave experience, their designs incorporate public icons alluding to colonial plantation slavery" (124). And to further support this theory, Gallant explains how these designs were, "employed widely in the abolitionists' public campaign of the 1780s" (124). In other words, Blake was most certainly influenced by the presence of slavery during the time of his writings. Given his various literary works which feature the presence of antislavery images and themes, it is safe to call Blake a devoted abolitionist.

Even though many during his time were uninterested in his views, some people today see Blake as a great social critic. Katey Castellano's article ""The Road of Excess Leads to the Palace of Wisdom": Alternative Economies of Excess in Blake's Continental Prophecies," she investigates the social criticism that led many to believe, "Blake [was] a radical" (Castellano 3). In fact, some labeled the visionary as being, "anti-rational" for his criticisms and statements (6). Castellano explains that some may have disregarded his writings, because of their powerful messages. For example, she feels that "Blake's Continental prophecies attempt to revitalize a type of radical religious dissent" (6). It is due to his radicalism that important figures may have viewed his works as threatening. On the other hand, it could also be that "Blake may have been intellectually and artistically disregarded by this radical circle on the basis of his class" (4). Either way, despite the reason, Blake's writings were often disregarded in their time. Oddly, his writings have risen sharply in popularity in the centuries following his death. Castellano notes, "modern scholars tend to view Blake as a man of genius, for both his poignant social criticism and his artistic ability" (4). Unlike before, where the public turned a blind eye to his writings and criticisms, present day scholars appreciate his harsh, yet abstract criticism. In addition, Blake's opinions are not exclusive to any one time period. With it being said that Blake, "vehemently opposes the progress of industrial capitalism and commodity," his stances and opinions can be used in numerous time periods in American history (6). Such examples include early 1900s labor practices, the expansion of oil empires, and the flourishing of present day consumerism that began in the mid twentieth century. The issues he found with society still persist today, with some select problems having exponentially worsened. The presence of these issues led him to be involved in what he deemed meaningful causes both inside and outside of his works.

While Blake's poetry features abolitionist images and terms, he was also dedicated to the cause outside of his writings. Within Britain, such a stance would not be out of the ordinary, because many citizens had supported the movement. In fact, Gallant explains how, "ordinary middle-class citizens, dissenters, working-class laborers across England as well as Scotland and Ireland..." were aligning themselves with the abolitionist movement (Gallant 123). Given its wide reach around the British islands, it seems to be a relatively well accepted stance. As for Blake, he, "was involved in London abolitionist circles. He attended the meetings of the Swedenborgians during 1791-2 as they planned their own colony of ex-slaves in Sierra Leone" (123). His understanding of both owned and liberated slaves' issues is broad, especially given that he was aware of slavery related events in Africa. Gallant further states that "he attended Joseph Johnson's weekly dinners, which usually included abolitionist sympathizers" (123). With such a great amount of information being gathered about slavery, Blake could not help but think of the matter as urgent or critical. He was so passionate about the issue that some thought, "his opposition to slavery was more radical than most of the abolitionists who had gone underground" (123). In fact, with his dedication to the stance against slavery, Blake did not retreat underground but rather made his opinions public by putting them in his writings. Gallant explains how his views are, "encoded in his works of 1793 and 1794 with their private mythology and oddly named characters" (124).

Various traits can be linked to slavery and even the emotions of the slaves themselves. For example, some of these works contain a blatant lack of hope. Because of this, Gallant believes, "the hopelessness he expresses was probably the slave's most common response to slavery" (128). Furthermore, Blake's inclusion of opinions, themes and terms sympathizing with abolitionism was not where his understanding of slavery ended. He felt that a commitment to slavery would result in severe punishment, especially for the nations who still relied upon slave labor. According to Gallant, he most likely, "believed that slave-trading nations would be visited with a divine and cataclysmic retribution" (129). In fact, "many considered the Saint-Domingue revolt to be terrifying but predictable because of the long history of planters' violence against their slaves" (129). In other words, given the events surrounding Saint-Domingue, many felt that this extreme punishment was not only coming, but that it was also predictable. Turning his attention to the American colonies, Blake included slavery and liberation in his prophetic works. Gallant states that "grapes imply liberation near the end of *America: A Prophecy*" (125). She also states that he alludes to slavery in his, "works that spanned the long war following the revolt" (130). Blake felt, after the American Revolutionary War, that the liberation of slaves and an end to slavery was possible. However, despite his views and hopes, history books would instead be filled with vast amounts of slavery that continues on for ages.

Given his strict opposition to slavery in all its forms, Blake would most likely heavily criticize the United States as it is in present day. In his article titled "William Blake's *America*," Mark Edmundson points out our modern day slavery and relates it to the slavery witnessed in Blake's time. According to Edmundson, the bulk of today's people exist as slaves, except the imagery has been greatly improved by the presence of feigned happiness and pleasantness. At one point, it was imagined that America had a brilliant workforce, where people cherished the work they did and received decent wages. These were not simply wages that provided just enough to scrape by, but instead were wages in which a person could live a life of moderate leisure. However, the reality is much more worse, and the bulk of the American people are regularly exploited for the good of the few. Edmundson explains:

> "Amid blazing wealth, great numbers of American children do not get enough to eat. Perhaps they are not starving, but they are hungry. The food they do get is overprocessed junk, which will in time make them sick. They live in horrible dwellings, both in the country and in the city. They go to bad schools, where there are few or no books, and where the teachers are overworked and overwhelmed. Many American children are as trapped in their own lived as the poor chimney sweeps were trapped in theirs. There is simply no better place for them to go" (Edmundson).

Similar to the poverty stricken chimney sweeps and underage prostitutes of Blake's time, many of our citizens are essentially trapped in their environments. They are held prisoner by a well structured system of difficult to pay debts. Upon reviewing their situations, many come to find that are only two real options available: work hard and perform the requested labor in hopes that life will someday become enjoyable and rewarding, or simply to die. While there are only a few ways to improve one's life if stuck in this situation, death can come in a number of ways as a result of poverty. Examining present day America reveals a variety of ways to die: many are unable to afford proper health care and eventually die once they get sick enough; some are forced to eat terrible foods and live in poor conditions either due to extremely low income or homelessness; others spend long hours at difficult jobs that may expose them to harmful chemicals or cause serious physical injuries. The ways in which the poorest half of the nation can die are never in short supply. Edmundson stresses that, while this is happening, "rich Americans plunder the nation, taking all they can get and then diving in for more" (Edmundson). Similar to Blake's time period, many live under the control of an astoundingly rich upper class that pays little attention to their concerns, and may not even care at all. Even the middle class, a tier of living still far beyond that of poverty, lives well enough to function in a state of fully blissful ignorance. Edmundson states that, in present day America:

> "There is no draft, so that the children of the middle class can avoid service and the middle class itself can neglect to think about the war at all, if it wishes. Middle-class people can go on seeking success and prosperity for themselves and their children, without considering our wars: They can live, unbothered, in the alluring but ultimately ruinous state of the Selfhood" (Edmundson).

Again, this heavily relates to not just American society, but also that of Blake's. In time periods both past and present, much of a nation's poor march off to fight the battles of the upper class. At best, middle and upper class citizens are involved in wars not at an infantry level, but at a middle to high ranking position of command. For example, the poor enlist in the military and often function at the level of private, corporal or potentially even as high as sergeant. However, on the other hand, upper class enlistees who can pay for officer training and military colleges often find themselves holding positions such as lieutenant, major or colonel. Of course, unless there is an accident of extreme rarity, none of these positions ever see actual combat. Meaning, to put it crudely, they are never in the cross hairs of an enemy. In conclusion, Blake would have most likely heavily criticized our society for its treatment of the poor and its rebranding of slavery. The reality that some experience more freedom and power because they were born into a wealthier family most certainly did and would still anger Blake. Focusing on the present, Blake would find himself in an odd position in regards to dominance, control and slavery given not merely their enduring presence, but their ability to transform and take on new shapes.

Blake is known to have both evaluated the past and pondered about the future in regards to slavery, and evidence of this act is found in his works. For example, in *America: A Prophecy*, he included elements of the past.

However, it may also be the case that he predicted the future in a relatively accurate manner. Given that a prophecy is a prediction of the future, it is safe to say that Blake was making an honest attempt to guess the future in portions of *America*. Blake knew that slavery came in multiple forms, such as chimney sweeps and farm workers, so it is no wonder that he may have predicted future enslavement to revolutionary forms of weaponry.

Since the early days of civilization, humans have exploited other humans by using them as slaves in one form or another. Threatened with punishment and even death, slaves worked for their masters and performed the jobs that provided the dominant society with large sums of money, convenience and other higher standards of living. However, in modern times, slavery has been revolutionized, because there is no longer any need for a great amount of masters and slavers to oversee tasks. Instead, dominant cultures have developed ways to ensure that other people do their bidding: by threatening complete and total obliteration. Essentially, it is the ultimate form of slavery, because lesser cultures do not need to be occupied or even visited. Put simply, either the wishes of the dominant culture are obeyed, or there is the potential for extreme destruction. The advanced weaponry and resulting enslavement to which Blake refers may actually be intercontinental ballistic missiles, or nuclear arms.

In *America: A Prophecy*, Blake uses imagery that many Americans would readily associate with nuclear weaponry. First, Blake mentions that "America faints" (Blake 21). When American soldiers first witnessed the nuclear device "Trinity," the first ever nuke, many of them were in complete awe. Despite the fact that many of them had seen combat, deaths and sights almost unimaginable to those outside of the military, Trinity left men speechless. Blake then mentions how, "Enraged the zenith grew" (21). A zenith is the highest point of an arc, so to suggest that it is growing means that the overall length of the arc is growing. This statement could relate to the arc-shaped trajectories of nuclear missiles flying long distances towards the enemies of America. Also, given that the growing zenith is a result of rage, it explains why, "human blood" shoots, "its veins all around the orbed heaven" (22). If the heavens to which Blake refers are the skies, this statement may mean that our targets would be many and distant. Blake then writes, "Intense, naked, a Human fire, fierce glowing as the wedge / Of iron heated in the furnace" (25-26). In this passage, there is much hidden meaning. The fires of a nuclear weapon are certainly intense and bridge, and they are exposed and unable to be hidden. They are the creation of not mythical gods, but humans, and this fact may explain why he refers to the sight as a "Human fire." Nature never created these weapons, humans did. Also, the use of "wedge" to describe the sight results in a dual meaning. A cloud whose width far exceeds its height is often referred to as a wedge cloud, meaning that it is quite wide. His choice of words describes a used nuclear device. Also, after the device has detonated, there would remain the iconic "towers" that Blake mentions (27). Long after the light of the bomb has faded, a tall tower of darkly colored dust usually remains above the scene. Blake then moves onto further description of the nuclear device and its appearance.

Blake continues describing the nuclear device in ways that are strikingly accurate. He states that "Surrounded; heat but not light went through the murky atmosphere. / The King of England looked westward trembling at the vision" (Blake 28-29). His description of the resulting shock wave from the blast is accurate. After the blast, anyone and anything in the vicinity of the shock wave is surrounded by intense heat. Even though the light from a nuclear weapon is brighter than the sun for a moment, it only briefly exists. What is most damaging to anything nearby is the shock wave that carries with it the intense heat. In addition, upon seeing this device being used, many other foreign leads did tremble to an extent, even if privately. The usage of atomic weaponry sent a message to the world that the United States was arguably the new dominant society. Essentially, as witnessed with Japan, a failure to follow orders from the United States meant the threat of total obliteration. Its existence made those without it slaves to those who did. Continuing onward, Blake further describes the event of the blast and relates it to mythology. He explains, "The terror like a comet, or more like the planet red / That once enclosed the terrible wandering comes in its sphere" (31-32). Blake's description of the nuclear weapon in flight is accurate, because a rocket closely mirrors the appearance of a comet: a bright, glowing spot in the sky trailed by a long tail of debris. The mention of the Mars-like "crimson disc" may bring mythology into his description of the event. His choice of Mars is appropriate, because red not only relates to rage, but also for Mars' association with war. Lastly, there is an emphasis on the number "three" in the passage (33). Many who witnessed the bomb compared it to the power of creation. In fact, with the name of the first device being "Trinity," the actual builders of the bomb did so as well. Blake's description of a weapon that would not be developed for over two centuries is accurate in many ways: its usage, its look, the perception of witnesses, and the responses of foreign leaders. Unfortunately, he was also accurate in regards to how it altered human life.

Where Blake's description of the bomb is accurate, his prediction of how it would affect the enslavement of people was backwards. In one portion of the text, Blake states that "The grave is burst," and there would be clay covering up, "The bones of death," and these descriptions of after the detonation are correct (Blake 38-39). However, where he seems to be completely backwards is his prediction for what the bomb would mean for the human race. He states, "Let the slave grinding at the mill run out into the field; / Let him look up into the heavens and laugh in the bright air" (42-43). Despite the accuracy of Blake's previous predictions, the bomb did not have this effect on people. It is fair to say that is was the complete opposite. Of course, with Blake's love for revolution and hatred for slavery, he would have wanted the creation of the bomb to be a positive event. Unfortunately, instead of being greeted as a liberating force, it bound the public and made them slaves to their own creation. Even though the device had been born from imagination and predicted to be used to end enslavement, the game changed once its design spread to the Soviet Union and our own creation could be used against us. Actually, if an American citizen had stopped working their long hours to look up into the sky and witness a nuclear missile in flight, it would have not brought thoughts of joy, but instead absolute terror. The Cuban Missile Crisis is a great example of how nuclear weapons brought the entire world to a standstill as a result of the near use of these weapons. What the public experienced was less of bliss and more close to paralyzing fear. Plus, it is highly doubtful that the liberation in which Blake spoke referred to death. The resulting release from long work hours and economic slavery sounds pleasant at first, but it is important to remember that human beings were what gave the world meaning in the eyes of Blake. After all, he did state, "Where man is not, nature is barren" (68). In conclusion, perhaps Blake knew of how gruesome and violent the use of these weapons would be, but was simply expressing his radically different views of revolution and liberation. Yet, there are very few instances in which the case be made for nuclear weapons being a liberating force as opposed to one meant solely for the long distance enslavement of others.

To date, every nation that has ever entered the small family of countries with nuclear arms has both used the weapons for enslavement and to avoid being enslaved. A recent example of a country seeking to avoid enslavement is North Korea. After the swift falls of the Iraqi and Afghani governments, North Korean leaders vowed to never experience the same fate. After witnessing the power and authority of nations who possessed nuclear arms, their government decided that the only way to avoid being toppled and enslaved by outside forces was to develop nuclear weapons. As a result of having nuclear weapons, countries such as South Korea and the United States could no longer easily conquer and control them. Even though it was done by developing weapons of mass destruction, the argument can be made that the North Korean government has successful liberated itself from the threat of slavery by outside forces. Moreover, similar cases can be made for every country that has created nuclear weapons. Similar to Blake's ideas, the possession of nuclear weapons does have the potential to liberate.

However, what was not predicted by Blake is their being used to enslave dozens of other countries. Especially given his radical intolerance for slavery and his pro-abolition stance, he probably would have not wanted to see nuclear arms used in a manner which results in the control and coercion of others. For Blake, violence through revolution and imaginative freedom were acceptable, but the enslavement and control of others was not. With Blake's possible prediction of the use of nuclear arms cast aside, present day America allows for a hefty amount of examination due to its uses of slavery.

Upon reviewing current events related to control and slavery both recent and moderately dated, there is much that Blake would have hated and loved. The aforementioned issue of economic and financial slavery is a problem that would have upset Blake, especially given its relationship with his time period. The eras are similar in that a very small portion of the population not only controls the lower classes, but also that the top tier of the population own a substantial amount of money. Take the recent recession for example, with powerful banking and investing companies creating intentionally difficult to comprehend loan agreements and convincing people that they can borrow far more than they could ever hope to repay. There is essentially no difference between present day corporate practices and the bad habits of the aristocracy during Blake's time. In addition, another example of modern slavery is the working class in its entirety. The working class, or the tier in between the middle class and poverty that must work to make ends meet, is typically in a stagnant state of working overtime in harsh conditions. Even though the working class is now able to experience a mild amount of leisure in their lives, showing that conditions have become better over the last two centuries, it is still slavery. The ownership class, or the tier above the upper class, remains at just a small percentage of our population, yet they control the wealth and require those who wish to make just above minimum wage to perform hard labor. After examining the similarities to Blake's time, the working class and their reliance on credit cards and borrowed money is still slavery, it has just taken on a different form. Lastly,

157

Blake may have disagreed with some aspects of modern behavior. In "Writ(h)ing Images. Imagination, the Human Form, and the Divine in William Blake, Salman Rushdie, and Simon Louvish," by Axel Stahler, Blake's criticism of morality and behavior are the focus. According to Stahler, he thought that heretics were, "whoever preaches rigid moral laws and follows the letter but not the spirit" (97). To Blake, our focus on tough morals and good behavior is keeping us from truly freeing our spirits and acting out. With that being said, he may have approved of the rebellious teen crowd more than he would have the strict older generations. Aside from what Blake may have disliked, there are issues that rest somewhere in between positivity and negativity.

Certain current events are usually regarded as either good or bad, but there are some issues that rest in the gray area in between the two. For example, the wars in Iraq and Afghanistan. After American forces liberated the two from various kinds of dictatorships, they remained behind and occupied the nations. It is difficult to say how Blake would feel about the issue. Considering his support of antislavery, it is possible that he would have supported the freedom of the two nations, but wanted for there to be no extended occupation. Similar questions arise when examining the CIA-led revolutions of Central America as well. Whether or not all revolutions are equal, especially considering the revolutions in question were not truly supported by the people, is subject to debate. Modern issues such as these are difficult to dissect, because it is not possible to examine them and wholeheartedly choose a side. Moving onward, there are issues that Blake would have most likely enjoyed to see.

Of the many recent issues that could be analyzed, no others compare to the recent waves of uprisings and revolts found in the Middle East and Africa. Within weeks of each other, Tunisia, Egypt, Yemen, Libya, Syria and others found themselves in a state of revolution. People took to the streets, sometimes violently, to push for better leadership and living conditions. To see people in nations coming together in order to free themselves from oppression would have most likely pleased Blake. The loss of life witnessed in the revolutions is unfortunate, but Blake felt that violent revolutions were positive and beneficial to humans. With his interest in antislavery and support of revolutions, these conflicts in the Muslim world may have been of great interest to Blake.

If Blake were alive today and gave his opinions on matters such as revolutions, the American public would find themselves both agreeing and disagreeing with his stances. The American people typically enjoy revolutions when it means better results for the United States. For example, in Libya, their revolts meant the threatening of a hated dictator and his style of leadership. Also, in Hollywood movies and television shows, the American people tend to romanticize revolution. Like Blake, the bloodshed and loss of human life is worth the benefits of freedom in the end. On the other hand, there are instances where Americans would probably find themselves in a disagreement with Blake. Given their breaking free from a crippling economic depression, Blake may have sympathized with Nazi Germany and the Soviet Union. Both nations' uprisings consisted of people seeking to change their governments at any cost. With that being said, it may appear to modern Americans that his love for revolution runs far too deep, and possibly ventures into irrationality. Another example is the Syrian revolts, which were filled with gruesome violence and murder. Perhaps there is a point where there has been enough violence, and revolutions begin to lose their good image. Unfortunately, given Blake's aforementioned beliefs, his love for freedom would have most likely outweighed his love for human life, which says a lot about his passions. In conclusion, after reviewing recent historical events, it is probable that Blake would have found contemporary America and its relations to be interesting to interpret.

If Blake were able to review America's history after writing *America: a Prophecy*, he would most likely enjoy the fact that our military has violently liberated other nations, but may also hate our inability to stop enslaving the poor, and becoming slaves ourselves. Since it is difficult to pick and choose a side considering modern times and the vast complexities by which they are surrounded, Blake may have found himself torn between issues. However, what reigns supreme above all is his disapproval of the enslavement of others, whether it is financially, physically, or even mentally. Similar to his own simultaneous dedication to British abolitionism and awareness of Caribbean and Asian forced labor at the hands of the empire, Blake would be stuck criticizing and praising various events. For the most part, considering his love of revolution and liberation, he would be pleased with America's history of freeing others at any cost, even if the results are pain, suffering and bloodshed. The glory of freedom and freeing are far outweighed by the pleasures of control and enslavement.

SOURCES

Blake, William. *America: A Prophecy. Blake: The Complete Poems*. Ed. W. H. Stevenson. New York: Longman, 2007. 193-212. Print.

Blake, William. *The Marriage of Heaven and Hell. Blake: The Complete Poems*. Ed. W. H. Stevenson. New York: Longman, 2007. 106-129. Print.

Castellano, Katey. ""The Road of Excess Leads to the Palace of Wisdom": Alternative Economies of Excess in Blake's Continental Prophecies." *Papers on Language & Literature* 42.1 (2006): 3-24. *MLA Bibliography*. Web. 26 Apr. 2011.

Edmundson, Mark. "William Blake's *America*." *Chronicle of Higher Education* 57.10 (2010). *MLA Bibliography*. Web. 26 Apr. 2011.

Elliott, Clare. "William Blake and America: Freedom and Violence in the Atlantic World." *Comparative American Studies* 7.3 (2009): 209-224. *MLA Bibliography*. Web. 26 Apr. 2011.

Gallant, Christine. "Blake's Antislavery Designs for *Songs of Innocence and of Experience*." *Wordsworth Cycle* 39 (2008): 123-130. *MLA Bibliography*. Web. 26 Apr. 2011.

Kripal, Jeffrey. "Reality Against Society: William Blake, Antiomianism, and the American Counterculture." *Common Knowledge* 13.1 (2006): 98-112. *MLA Bibliography*. Web. 26 Apr. 2011.

Stahler, Axel. "Writ(h)ing Images. Imagination, the Human Form, and the Divine in William Blake, Salman Rushdie, and Simon Louvish." *English Studies* 89.1 (2008) 94-117. *MLA Bibliography*. Web. 26 Apr. 2011.

18. Contrasting Behaviors of Minor Characters in Stephen Crane's *The Monster*

Man in Hindsight

Aside from the story's major characters, Stephen Crane's *The Monster* contains many equally important minor characters. Dr. Trescott's son, Jimmie, has a number of functions in the tale, and helps to illuminate the theme through his actions. In the beginning of the tale, Jimmie is polite, yet after the fire he is rude and hurtful to Henry Johnson. Before the fire, Jimmie does not lie to his father, and fears being punished. However, after the fire, Jimmie is not so truthful with his father, and even tells half-truths in response to his father's questions. In addition, Jimmie ceases conversing with Henry Johnson after the fire, and ends their friendship. Instead of being a decent friend, Jimmie only uses Henry Johnson for insulting games. These contrasting behaviors are the result of Jimmie changing after the fire occurs. Another function Jimmie serves is to show how he can heal after the fire injures him, while Henry Johnson is unable. The second character who illuminates the theme through her functions is Ms. Farragut. Even though she used to love Henry Johnson quite a bit, and would try her best to look good for him, she grows to hate him. By the end of the novella, she is unable to even look at Henry Johnson's face. Furthermore, for both Jimmie and Ms. Farragut, there is no intimacy left in their friendships with Henry Johnson. In Stephen Crane's *The Monster*, Jimmie and Ms. Farragut's function is to illuminate the theme of contrast by their actions both before and after the fire which engulfs Dr. Trescott's house.

The major theme of Stephen Crane's novella, *The Monster*, is contrast. Aside from Jimmie and Ms. Farragut, other minor characters help to illuminate the theme of contrast in the story. For example, Mrs. Farragut transforms from being an accepting and polite woman to being easily frightened. Additionally, the townspeople as a whole fit this mold as they all make the transition from being mostly accepting to being hurtful, hateful and irrationally rejecting of Henry Johnson. With the differing behaviors both before and after the fire comes an undeniably strong contrast.

Dr. Trescott's young son, Jimmie, serves to illuminate the theme of contrast in many ways. In the very first paragraph of the tale, Jimmie is described as being a young and innocent child. He enjoys spending time in the garden, playing with toy trains and pretending to be a somewhat careless conductor. He accelerates the train until it is at a dangerous rate of speed, and, "...a wheel of his cart [destroys] a peony" (Crane 190). The result of this incident is a young boy who is speechless, and fearful of his father's punishment. The grave fear becomes evident when, "...the whole thing had taken away the boy's vocabulary" (Crane 191). The function of this minor character's moment of fear and innocence is to create contrast with his later forms of entertainment.

As the novella progresses, Jimmie undergoes a transition which renders him absentminded to the ways he has become. Rather than simply playing with trains, Jimmie decides to play with Henry Johnson in a hurtful manner. He and the and other boys within his gang play a game which consists of seeing who is brave enough to walk up to the monstrously hideous Henry Johnson and touch him (Crane 236). When Jimmie is asked by Dr. Trescott what it is he and the others are doing, Jimmie responds with the half-truth, "We was playin'" (238). When his father asks him a second time, he responds again with, "Just playin'" (238). At this moment, Jimmie seems as if he is a different child altogether. As opposed to honestly answering his father, he would rather respond with generalized and somewhat deceitful comments. Clearly, he does not want his father to find out what it is he was doing with the other boys and Henry Johnson. Furthermore, it is evident that Jimmie is absentminded, and forgets his trusting relation with his father. No matter what the age, Jimmie undergoes an unacceptable transition.

To Jimmie, Henry Johnson was once a great friend, as opposed to a subject of rude games. Before the facially damaging fire, Jimmie would commonly spend time with Henry Johnson as he washed Dr. Trescott's buggy (192). Moreover, Henry Johnson, "...grinned fraternally when he saw Jimmie coming" (192). Jimmie was seen as a brother to Henry Johnson, and he was someone to be trusted. Henry Johnson trusted Jimmie to such as degree, that he would even let Jimmie wash one of the wagon wheels on occasion. In addition, while the devastating fire engulfs Dr. Trescott's house, their friendship is at its peak as Henry Johnson is Jimmie's primary rescuer. Despite the frightening possibility of being burned alive, Henry Johnson goes, "...in after the kid" (207). This very action, above all else, illustrates how deep their friendship was both before and during the fire. However, there is contrast in the fact that Jimmie no longer speaks with Henry Johnson after the fire. Furthermore, Jimmie's absentmindedness is revealed yet again as he forgets the friendship they both once shared.

Henry Johnson's rescue of Jimmie sets him apart from the townspeople. While most all of the townspeople stood and watched the fire destroy Dr. Trescott's house, Jimmie was stuck inside and left with the chance of a painful death. When it was learned that Jimmie was still inside, Henry Johnson rushed into the house and looked for him. Jimmie's involvement in the fire displays another important function of his within the novella: to give Henry Johnson's inner character a chance to show. When Henry Johnson is notified by Mrs. Trescott that Jimmie is still inside, "He [plunges] past her and [disappears]..." (202). If Jimmie's life were never threatened, Henry Johnson would not have had that chance to display his inner courage and bravery. Additionally, Henry Johnson's good deed is amplified by the gravity of the inferno. The fire which enveloped Dr. Trescott's house was so dangerous, that many of the townspeople assumed that "Jimmie Trescott and Henry Johnson had been burned to death..." (209). Therefore, to a large degree, Jimmie's life threatening situation illuminates Henry Johnson's true character.

An important function of Jimmie is to display how he is healed, while Henry Johnson is not. After the fire, both Jimmie and Henry Johnson are left with burns which require medical attention. Furthermore, Jimmie's wounds heal somewhat quickly, and he is, "...sufficiently recovered..." (212). In addition, he also gets to carry on with his life and, "...pay a visit to his grandparents in Connecticut" (212). Unfortunately, Henry Johnson is not so lucky as his wounds leave him permanently damaged, and he is left looking unattractive. There is a great deal of contrast between the two characters after the fire as Jimmie continues living his comfortable life, and Henry Johnson's life within the town changes altogether. The injuries due to the fire greatly illuminate the theme of contrast within the tale.

Another character who greatly illuminates the theme of contrast within Crane's *The Monster* is Ms. Farragut. Before the fire destroyed Henry Johnson's face, she would try to look good for him when he visited her house. For example, when he visits Ms. Farragut the first time in the story, she is, "...scrambling wildly into her best gown" (197). This sentence indirectly reveals a great deal of information about their relationship before the fire took place. She is not simply putting a dress on, but is actually scrambling to get into it. This action exposes her anxiety and nervousness in the presence of Henry Johnson. Moreover, she decides to put on the best dress she owns, as opposed to a dress of typical quality. Ms. Farragut tries her best to look as good as she can for Henry Johnson, displaying how much she loves him. After the fire, she would rather stay in basic attire and does not care much for his company.

There is a great deal of contrast between how Ms. Farragut treats Henry Johnson before and after the fire in terms of intimacy. After Henry Johnson arrives and speaks to Mrs. Farragut while Ms. Farragut readies herself, he is invited inside their home. Ms. Farragut loves him enough to speak with him for an extended period of time within her very own living room. After the visit is completed and Henry Johnson leaves, Ms. Farragut asks her mother, "Oh, ma, isn't her divine?" (197). She clearly loves him a great deal, and seeks the approval of her mother. However, after the fire, Ms. Farragut cares nothing for Henry Johnson at all. At first sight, she falls to the ground and begins to crawl towards her house as if she were fleeing to safety. Rather than recognizing him as a good friend, Ms. Farragut labels him as being, "...a monster..." (228). Additionally, she does not put on a wonderful dress as a result of Henry Johnson's visit, or treat him with respect. She cares nothing for trying to impress the so-called monster who stands before her. Contrastingly, she also cares nothing for Henry Johnson's exterior beauty after the fire. Instead of looking at Henry Johnson and acknowledging him, "She shielded her eyes with her arms and tried to crawl past it..." (229). Ms. Farragut treats hims as if he is a threat, and forgets the relationship they used to have. When comparing these two scenes from before and after the fire, there is a great deal of contrast as Ms. Farragut forgets the past, and what Henry Johnson meant to her.

In *The Monster*, by Stephen Crane, the minor characters Jimmie and Ms. Farragut perform functions that breathe life into the theme of contrast. Jimmie undergoes a transition from being a kind and caring friend, to a bully who only associates with Henry Johnson through terrible games. The gravity of the friendship with Henry Johnson in which Jimmie leaves behind is displayed by the intense fire he is rescued from. In addition, Ms. Farragut's actions after the fire largely contrast her actions from before the fire occurred. She and Jimmie are revealed to have changed for the worst, and their new behaviors are very different than their old behaviors. Unlike Henry Johnson, who seems to remain the same on the inside throughout the story, both Jimmie and Ms. Farragut change drastically. It is because of these contrasting behaviors that Jimmie and Ms. Farragut are equally as important as the major characters within the novella.

SOURCE

Crane, Stephen. "The Monster." *Great Short Works of Stephen Crane*. New York: Perennial, 2004. 190-247.

19. Comparing Sins in J. M. Synge's *The Tinker's Wedding*

The Social Structure of Man

In *The Tinker's Wedding*, by J. M. Synge, the theme of sinning is incredibly prevalent. Throughout the play, the tinkers commit every one of the seven deadly sins. However, unfortunately for the image of the Catholic church, the priest does the same. The only two sins which the tinkers truly dominate are lust and wrath. Other than those two, the priest either matches the tinkers in their amount of sinning, or completely dominates the category altogether. It is a truly sad sight as the priest should not be committing any sins whatsoever. Committing far less sins than the tinkers in any category is still a complete defeat as the priest has no business being sinful. In Synge's *The Tinker's Wedding*, the priest is much more evil than the tinkers not simply for the sins he commits, but also for the fact that he is a member of the church while committing them.

The deadly sin of envy appears in *The Tinker's Wedding* less than the others, but still plays an important role. Although Sarah Casey wants to be married in order to gain dignity and be viewed as respectable in the eyes of society, there is envy in her words. It is indisputable that Sarah Casey is envious of those who are married. She is envious, because those who are married have what she does not: respect and honor. However, not surprisingly, the priest commits more envious acts than the tinkers. Throughout the play, he makes it known that he is envious of both the tinkers and the bishop. He envies the tinkers' lifestyle and freedom. They are not committed to responsibilities, unlike the priest who travels, "...east and west for a sick call..." (Synge 189). The priest also envies the bishop's power. The bishop is a higher member of the church than he is, and has much more power than the priest. While Sarah Casey is mildly envious of those who are married, the envy committed by the priest overshadows that of the tinkers.

In *The Tinker's Wedding*, pride is a major problem for the priest.

166

While the tinkers are not completely immune to pride, the majority of pride demonstrated in the play comes from the priest. The reader is exposed to pride from the tinkers when Sarah first speaks to the priest. She mentions that she is, "...the Beauty of Ballinacree" (Synge 185). Sarah finds herself to be extraordinarily beautiful, and mentions her title as if it is going to move her up in society. Unfortunately for her, it does not. However, the priest is the same as he is very full of pride, and it does not benefit him whatsoever as well. From the moment we first meet the priest he believes as if he is above the tinkers, and comes across as being a snob. It is inexcusable for a priest to act this way, and especially to the poverty stricken. In addition, it is important to remember, according to David H. Greene and Edward M. Stephens' *J. M. Synge, 1871-1909*, "*The Tinker's Wedding*, it must be emphasized, is not a play about the common people of Ireland" (Greene 182). The tinkers are poor, socially ignorant and supposedly godless people, and the priest is fully committed to the church and its teachings. These four people are not your average citizens. Though the priest looks down on the tinkers for being without God, it is debatable that the tinkers do not believe in a higher power. For example, Alan Price explains that "...the tinkers are bound up with the natural world instead of institutionalized religion" (Price 15). In other words, though the three tinkers may not believe in one form of religion, it does not mean they do not have their own unique spirituality. Therefore, though the priest would disagree, there is not much separating them from one another. Weldon Thornton explains this fact in *J. M. Synge and the Western Mind*, "*The Tinker's Wedding* focuses directly upon 'cultural relativism' by depicting a contrast between the world view of the tinkers and that of the priest" (Thornton 156). In truth, the tinkers and the priest are not too different from each other, and their differences are more minimal than the play suggests. Given this fact, there is no need for pride to come from anybody.

Both the tinkers and the priest enjoy committing the deadly sin of sloth in *The Tinker's Wedding*. However, with the tinkers the case is much less severe. Michael is usually hard at work making cans and other items out of tin. Additionally, even though it is not exactly honest work, Michael and Sarah spend time together stealing from the neighbors. The only tinker who is guilty of indulging in sloth is Mary. She regularly sleeps until noon and lingers around for the rest of the day. The only task she does which can be seen as work is walking to the nearest tavern at night. However, all three tinkers cannot compare to the priest when it comes to sloth. The priest does not have much to do, yet hates doing it. The priest explains to Mary, "It's a hard life, I'm telling you, a hard life, Mary Byrne..." (Synge 189-190). Not only does he hate his duties as priest, but he even fails in helping save the souls of the tinkers. Here we have a group of three secular tinkers who are without God, and are surely doomed to an eternity in Hell, but the priest does not help. The reason for this is his snobbish nature, and the fact that it would take too much effort to help.

The priest has a severe problem with both greed and avarice throughout the play. Though the man is a priest, he withholds the sacrament of marriage from the couple until they provide compensation. Early in the play, the priest asks Sarah Casey the question, "Is it marry you for nothing at all?" (Synge 186). His focus is clearly on monetary gain, and this is the case towards the end of the play. When the priest discovers the bag containing empty bottles, he withholds the sacrament of marriage once more (Synge 198). Despite the fact that he cannot keep two people from getting married, he should not be demanding a large amount of money from such a poor couple. He understands the tinkers are poor, and requiring money for free services is unethical. When he realizes the tinkers cannot provide the demanded amount of money, he settles for what little they can provide: their cans (Synge 187). As if taking money was not bad enough, he takes one of the few things that can make the tinkers money. Another way the priest shows his greedy nature is through gambling. The priest often gambles when visiting with his friends from high society, and the tinkers notice this as it is a common occurrence (Synge 184). Moreover, the priest's greed is universal and does not just apply to money. It is mentioned that he has a large stomach, showing that he greedy when it comes to food as well (Synge 184). The sin of avarice, which is never having enough, pairs well with greed, and the priest is guilty of this as well. When Sarah Casey offers the priest ten shillings, it is simply not enough for him. He demands more money, and states, "If it's ten shillings you have, let you get ten more the same way, and I'll marry you then" (Synge 184). Both the priest and the tinkers seem equally greedy in *The Tinker's Wedding*, and that says a lot about the priest.

The tinkers have faults of their own in terms of greed as both Sarah and Michael love to steal from neighbors, and Mary always needs more money for drinking. When Mary begins to fall asleep, Sarah and Michael are off to steal from a local resident by the name of Tim Flaherty (Synge 193). Their greed drives the need to steal, and the fact that they both keep repeating the act shows they can never have enough. Mary Byrne is also greedy as she always needs more money for drinking. At one point, she asks Sarah to leave her, "...the two little coppers you have, the way I can walk up in a short while, and get another pint for my sleep" (Synge 193). Later in the play, her greed hits a new low as she steals the gallon can from Sarah and Michael and sells it for drinking money. When she finds out that the gallon can was to be used to pay for Sarah and Michael's wedding, she, "...[looks] at the bundle with surprise and dread" (Synge 201). Conclusively, the greed of the priest and tinkers is matched, as they are both completely driven by it.

The priest and the tinkers can not get enough food as well, as they are all gluttons. With the priest, this fact is more obvious as one of his more noticeable features is his large stomach (Synge 184). When the priest is first introduced, it is made known that he is very drunk, which is another form of gluttony (Synge 185). In fact, he is so drunk that Sarah Casey believes she can get a better price on her marriage. Also, he drinks when he sarcastically states, "Well, here's to your good health, and God forgive us all" (Synge 189). At this point, there is no denying the fact that the priest is a drunkard as he drinks alcohol right in front of them. The tinkers are also gluttons as they love to drink in excess. Though Sarah begs the priest to marry them before Mary drinks all of their money away (Synge 186), it is evident that they are all gluttonous drunkards by the end of the play. After the attempt at becoming married fails, there is nothing the tinkers would rather do than simply become drunk for the rest of their days. If there is any sin in which the characters of this play commit more than greed, it is gluttony.

One of two sins the tinkers commit far more than the priest is lust. They have sex out of wedlock, and there is proof of this through subtle facts in the play. First, both Sarah and Michael give in to their lust as they have sex before they are married. It is interesting to see such a disregard for standards, and Richard Tillinghast explains in his article for the Dublin Journal that there is a, "...pagan wildness of Irish life..." (Tillinghast 33). Evidence of this is found throughout the play as the tinkers live life freely, and without any concerns for morality. Second, it is evident this happens, because Sarah Casey is pregnant. One of the signs that Sarah Casey is pregnant is the ring not fitting. Though the ring used to fit, it seems to be too tight for Sarah's finger when she tries it on days later (Synge 182). Another sign is the mood swings and other differences in Sarah Casey, "...since the mood did change" (Synge 182). The significance in mentioning the moon is that it has a monthly cycle, and this relates to the woman's menstrual cycle. Sarah Casey is clearly pregnant, and this means that she and Michael have been giving in to lustful temptations. In addition, there is the issue of Sarah Casey being attracted to and threatening to leave Michael for Jaunting Jim (Synge 182-184). If she cannot get what she wants from Michael, she will simply leave him for another man she is attracted to.

The sin of lust should not apply to the priest, but it unfortunately does. While it is not confirmed that the priest makes physical contact with anyone, he does commit lust in his heart. For example, at one point, he looks at Sarah's face in a borderline lustful manner. Later in the play, the priest watches the girls outside of the church through the window (Synge 206). Both the tinkers and the priest are lustful, but what makes the priest's sin worse is the fact that he a member of the church. If there is anyone who should not be lustful, it is a priest rather than tinkers.

The only other sin the tinkers commit far more than the priest is wrath. Interestingly enough, the priest is never violent with anyone throughout the play. He is constantly either angry or in a bad mood, but does not come close to matching the wrath of the tinkers. Furthermore, the only point in which the priest seems to truly let loose is at the end when he screams curses at the tinkers in Latin. Other than that, he merely seems as if he is in a poor mood. However, the tinkers dominate this type of sin as they are always angry with one another. Sarah Casey and Mary Byrne can be seen constantly arguing throughout the entire play. Despite the fact that they wish to be married, Sarah and Michael argue quite a bit in the beginning of the play as well. At one point, Michael even threatens to strike Sarah (Synge 192). On the bright side, though the tinkers seem as if they are an angry and violent bunch, their violence is somewhat controlled as it stays within the group. The only time their violence physically effects others is at the very end of the play when they ride the priest while he is inside of the church. Even though David H. Greene explains that there is a "rage" which can be seen in the tinkers, the tinkers suppress their anger and never let it reach the point of extreme violence (Greene 824). While the priest matches and even surpasses the tinkers in most categories of sin throughout the play, wrath and lust are dominated by the tinkers.

There is something to be said about the nature of the play, and the date in which it would have been performed on stage if it could have been tolerated by the public. Although short lived, Synge was an incredibly popular and successful play write. However, *The Tinker's Wedding* is his one exception as it is his most unloved and unpopular work. David H. Greene notes in his article for the Modern Language Association, "...the Abbey Theater wisely avoided *The Tinker's Wedding*" (Greene 824). He goes as far as promoting the idea that the play has been, "...labeled an ugly duckling" (Greene 824). While it may first appear as if Greene is too critical of the play,

171

he explains how even Synge himself thought the play was, "...too immoral for Dublin" (Greene 824). It is important to remember not simply the subject matter, but the date and location in which this play was completed. Turn of the century Ireland was a country largely based around the rigid rules of catholicism, and this play would not have been graciously accepted by the public. This is a play which features a sinful and mean spirited catholic priest as one of its main characters. Realistically, performing such an offensive play in Ireland would be dangerous and certainly provoke riots. Greene continues his evaluation of The Tinker's Wedding with the statement, "Synge's only mistake was in publishing the results of his experiment" (Greene 824). Furthermore, not only does Greene believe that this is Synge's worst work, he also believes it should have never been made public. Although, there is one upside to Greene's article on Synge's supposed failure, and it is that the play, "...[includes], in an earlier version of the preface to the play an apology to the Irish clergy" (Greene 824). Therefore, Synge knew how offensive he was being in writing this play. Offensive subject matter or not, Synge exhibits a great deal of social awareness in the creation of The Tinker's Wedding.

The priest in Synge's The Tinker's Wedding is far more evil than the tinkers as he is a sinful member of the church. Such a thing as a sinful priest should not exist, and the fact it does is unfortunate. While the tinkers do commit many sins throughout the play, one could argue that their only crime is a lack of exposure to religion. The Tinker's Wedding forces readers to question whether or not the tinkers are evil when they are simply ignorant. However, the priest should be held more accountable for his sins as he is a member of the church. He is familiar with sins and how to rise above them, but chooses not to. Positions in society mean nothing as the priest is a drinking and gambling man with lustful temptations, and an absolute love for both money and power, instead of being humble and helpful

SOURCES
Green, David H. "*The Tinker's Wedding*, a Revaluation." *PMLA, Modern Language Association*. 62.3

(1947): 824.

Green, David H., and Edward M. Stephens. *J. M. Synge, 1871-1909*. New York: The Macmillan Company, 1959.

Price, Alan. *Synge and Anglo-Irish Drama*. London: Methuen & Co LTD, 1961.

Synge, John M. "The Tinkers Wedding." *The Complete Plays*. New York: Vintage Books, 1935. 181-209.

Thornton, Weldon. *J. M. Synge and the Western Mind*. New York: Harper & Row Publishers, Inc., 1979.

Tillinghast, Richard. "Wilde, Synge & Orpen." *The Dublin Journal*. 24 (2006): 33.

20. Relating Postsecular Properties in *The English Patient* and *The Matrix*

The Purpose of Man

Fluctuations in religiosity throughout history have provided for instances of both secularization and a return to the sacred. A handful of time periods qualify as being postsecular, but none more so than the ones centered in the twentieth century. There are a few terms which define a postsecular period of time. One such definition is a regained sense of purpose, or a reengagement in a fallen world. Some find it possible to see meaning in our lives, despite a world that once seemed to lack the sacred to the point where engagement was difficult and purpose seemed impossible. Others become distanced from the world and lose their sense of purpose, because they are seemingly left with no other choice. Two examples of these scenarios are found in the Wachowski Brothers' film *The Matrix* and Michael Ondaatje's novel *The English Patient*, respectively. Neo, the main character of *The Matrix*, slowly finds purpose in an otherwise meaningless life while *The English Patient*'s Almasy slowly loses his ability to stay engaged in the fallen world. Both worlds are terrible places with little point in living. Neo finds himself working at a job and going home to stay up all night pondering the deeper meaning of it all. On the other hand, what life Almasy had is ripped away from him piece by piece until he is a burn victim without a real purpose in life. For the most part, the two main characters' engagement in their fallen worlds and purposes reflect each other, with Neo realizing that he is the savior of the world and Almasy having his entire life stripped away from him. Despite their differing time periods, genres, formats and styles of delivery, *The English Patient* and *The Matrix* reveal each other as near opposites in terms of engagement in a fallen world and sense of purpose.

Through the revealing of Almasy's past, readers are provided with a looking glass into his once purposeful life. Caravaggio says to Hana, "there was a Hungarian named Almasy, who worked for the Germans during the war. He flew a bit with the Afrika Korps, but he was more valuable than that. In the 1930s he had been one of the great desert explorers" (Ondaatje 163). This passage is important, because it reveals much of Almasy's past and focuses on the two stages of his life before his accident: the period of time in which he was a desert cartographer, and the time he spent in the military. In the moment he transitions from one profession to the next, he becomes less involved in the world, because it slowly falls apart around him. Almasy's early life may first appear to be dull, but it was actually much more positive than it seems.

The wandering of Almasy through the desert may compare to Exodus, but the escapism in which he experienced was healthy and positive. In David Jasper's article "Wanderings in the Desert: From the Exodus to *The English Patient*," he lightly explores how Almasy had purpose and meaning in his life despite his travels throughout an arid environment. These deserts provided Almasy with healthy escapism, and allowed him to engage the world while still ignoring its greater negative aspects. For example, he is able to live his life, travel the desert and remain a skillful cartographer while simultaneously ignoring the world and its issues. Jasper explains, "Ondaatje is speaking, of course of the deserts of Egypt and the Sahara, which in Arabic means, roughly 'the brown void', but can also mean 'nothingness', a forgetting of the world" (Jasper 153). It may not be by accident that Ondaatje chose a location whose dual meaning is a forgetting of the world or nothingness. When thinking of the stereotypically lifeless desert, it is not uncommon to imagine a vast and empty expanse. In theory, this could relate to the clearing of Almasy's mind, allowing him to forget the troubles of the outside world. This understanding of location choice explains how he could remain focused and have a purpose in such a world. In a sense, he persistently searches and explores a world within a world; one so far removed from negative politics that it allows him to remain engaged. However, his life would soon begin to change.

Early in the chronological order of the novel, Almasy was the most involved and engaged in the fallen world. Despite the events surrounding World War I and how many regarded the world to be a fallen place since its end, Almasy was still engaged. He explored the treacherous Sahara desert in Africa, and was regarded as a talented cartographer, or mapper. He knew of many tribes, and could navigate environments that would kill others with ease. In addition, he also had a love interest that drove him to live. Love is a common reason for living, and such was the case for Almasy in regards to Katharine. Even though she was in a relationship with another man, Almasy still loved her and wanted to her to his own. Aside from his successful career, his love for her certainly gave him a sense of purpose. However, everything changed for the worst once the first of two major accidents occurred.

In *The English Patient*, characters experience disengagement from their world at the hands of accidents and suffering. Focusing on Almasy in particular, he experiences what is perhaps the greatest fall of any of the characters, and does so on multiple levels. Literally, Almasy does indeed suffer from an enormous fall, explaining, "I fell burning into the desert" (Ondaatje 5). But also abstractly, he comes crashing down into a harsh reality plagued by stasis and both physical and emotional pain. Even though he had lived an engaging and active lifestyle, he later loses all purpose and even identity after the accident. Earlier portions of the text illustrate his removal from the world, and how he is out of his element. He explains, after being picked up and cared for after his crash, "I didn't know their tribe" (5). In an environment he knows so much about, he is for once suffering from a lack of knowledge. In addition, he suffers from a loss of identity which is evident during the exchange, "Who are you? I don't know. You keep asking me. You said you were English" (5). His life, his understanding of the region and his identity all suffer as a result of his accident, leaving him with less purpose than he had before. Thanks to spontaneous community, he just sits there,

"He listens to her, swallowing her words like water" (5). And so begins his low quality life of laying in a bed, receiving treatments and listening to the conversation that fills the rooms. His life is stuck in a dark place, without purpose or a willingness to engage the world.

After the initial accident and Katharine's injury, Almasy found himself a situation that would remove all purpose or willingness to engage the world from his life. With Katharine hurt and dying, it was up to Almasy to get help and save her life. Unfortunately, he was unable to do so, because it was suspected that he was a spy. This crucial delay in rescue meant that Katharine was undoubtedly dead, and that the love of his life was gone forever. As if that were not enough, his job as a cartographer had been replaced with helping the Germans in World War II. His new job was not only unpleasant in comparison to his earlier career, but it also helped contribute to the further destruction of the already damaged world. With that being said, his grim outlook on life would only get worse as he experienced a second accident, a brutal plane crash, which would remove the last bit of meaning from his life of recent suffering. From that point on, he lived a life of removal and disengagement in the villa.

During his time at the villa, Almasy endures his physical pain and slowly experiences progressively lesser health. Greatly contrasting the newfound engagement in which Neo experiences in the later half of *The Matrix*, Almasy experiences a removal so great that he physically cannot take part in the world. Attempting to care for her patient, Hana only manages his wounds, but is unable to heal. She tries to help, "always there were ointments, or darkness, against his skin" (Ondaatje 9). However, despite the constant attention, her efforts only made his poor health slightly more enjoyable, if even at all. Additionally, his life became a matter of routines, similar to Neo's life early on. Hana narrates how, "he lay once more covered in cloth" (9). The lack of movement and activity suggest his inevitable death, because a lack of engagement paired with the resulting depression suggests a symbolic death. Hana further explains his lack of movement, saying how it

177

was clear that he, "should never be moved because of the fragility of his limbs" (51). As a result, it is in his bed that he stays, stuck and subject to a torturous downward spiral. Hana can only, "give him saline baths for the keloided skin and extensive burns" (51). Her inability to cure him and only manage his wounds demonstrates how he is essentially the living dead, or a man with no future. Without a future, there is little purpose, only the present. Somewhat showing how his impending death has been realized, Almasy often seemingly practices death. Being witness to this, Hana, "disliked his lying there with a candle in his hands, mocking a deathlike posture, wax falling unnoticed onto his wrist. As if he was preparing himself, as if he wanted to slip into his own death by imitating its climate and light" (62). With his death most likely realized, Almasy seems as if he fantasizes about peacefully dying and slipping away from this world. In other words, he is at a point in his life where he is about to experience the ultimate step towards disengagement and having no purpose.

To illustrate just how little purpose Almasy's life had towards the chronological end of the text, he provides us with descriptions of the highs and lows of his life. He explains that "*Death means you are in the third person*," showing that you are more of an object than human (Ondaatje 247). The objectification of Almasy shows how he is more closely related to the dead than the living, because the living are referred to by name while the dead are seen as mere bodies. Furthermore, he experiences such a low quality of living that it is explained how, "that summer the English patient wore his hearing aid so he was alive to everything in the house" (88). The difference between being more or less alive, or being engaged or disengaged, was the use of a hearing aid so one of his five senses would be better than it was before. His being referred to in the third person and terrible life indicate that he is one step from death in terms of disengagement with the world. Another way of putting his fall into perspective is to examine the contrast between start and finish.

Through the revealing of past events and their details, Almasy's life slowly takes shape throughout the novel. It is soon clear how he arrived at this situation, and from where he came. Andrew Shin's article "*The English Patient*'s Desert Dream" focuses on these events, but most importantly examines the transition in which the character experiences. At first, "Almásy is the romantic adventurer who cultivates alienation as a way to break out of the constraints and relationships that shape a life" (Shin 213). He has a strong sense of purpose in life, and is ready to engage the world. Shin understands his constant exploration of the desert to be, "Almásy's sustained fantasy of denationalization" (214). This theory holds truth, given that Almasy explores numerous tribes and travels over many of their territories. With that being said, "Ondaatje initially presents Almasy according to stereotypes of western power, authority, and mastery: he is the Royal Geographic Society cartographer who packages and hierarchizes space for Western consumption" (218). Early in his chronological history, he is full of power, ability and purpose. His specialty is the, "his ability to penetrate, circumscribe, and navigate desert space, activities inextricably intertwined with imperialist aggression" (218). However, despite these elite skills, Almasy's life transitions into a life of pain and sadness, only followed by yet more suffering. His pursuit of love and his addiction to discovery eventually prove to be, "lethal, sealing his own fate and dooming Katharine to an eerie death by entombment" (219). Without his love and being removed from his travels, he experiences a loss of purpose. To make matters worse, after retrieving Katharine's body, they are both, "brought crashing to earth, a fall from Paradise, in perhaps the novel's most memorable instance of descendental imagery" (219). Soon after, it is clear that Almasy is without all that he had before, except his ability to simply live. As Shin puts it, he experiences a, "fiery demise" (230). He is then ironically stationed at a place that has both experienced much activity and touched many lives. Shin explains the situation, stating, "as an image of human activity, life at the former cloister conflates sacred and human time, projecting a history of previous lives" (222). Unfortunately, Almasy rests uneasily within the compound and is unable to move freely or enjoy life. Looking back and examining the contrast between his earlier and present conditions illuminates the transition in which he has undergone. His earlier life was full of meaning and purpose, while his present condition leaves him with little chance to engage the fallen world in which he lives. Being placed inside a sacred place leaves him little comfort, and brings up the point of Almasy's faith.

Throughout the novel there is a stressing of the fact that they are inside a sacred place, but this point is of little comfort to a man whose outlook on life is so bleak. When it is stated that "it was a place of faith," the question remains: but a faith in what? There is no chance of survival, everything he loved is gone, and his life has no purpose, because he is a nearly lifeless cadaver (Ondaatje 139). This may be why he accepts his reality later in the text, stating, "it is important to die in holy places" (260). In other words, since he is going to die, it might as well be in a place that may lead to something better. It indirectly implies that there is nothing for him left in this world. Moreover, Almasy's situation points to the larger picture, that it is not just Almasy, the spontaneous community in the villa, or the region that is falling apart: it's the world. Late in the novel, there is mention of, "the death of a civilisation," and even the use of nuclear weapons to destroy entire cities (286). While Almasy has it the worst out of the characters, others and even people outside of the villa relate to his condition. They are stuck lingering in a world that is falling apart around them. Additionally, even the villa itself has seen better days in its past and is subject to a deterioration it has never before experienced. It is stated that "the staircase had lost its lower steps during the fire that was set before the soldiers left" (13). While the destruction of the villa may seem to be terrible, it is important to remember all that it has endured up until this point. It is explained in the text, "it was a hospital, she said quietly. Before that, long before that a nunnery. Then armies took it over" (56). However, at this point, it begins to slowly crumble around them, signifying how their present is subject to destruction so great. The people within the villa take notice, and some recognize how it relates the greater issue of global destruction. The many who notice this deterioration, like Almasy, begin to suffer from an unwillingness to engage the world as a result.

Continuing to expand the focus outward, as opposed to on the individual, reveals that the storyline of becoming removed from the world and losing one's sense of purpose applies to many people in a time of war. In his article "History and Story: Unconventional History in Michael Ondaatje's *The English Patient* and James A. Michener's *Tales of the South Pacific*," Madhumalati Adhikari explores what the novel says on a broader level. He feels that the novel attempts, "to modify our lives and the lives of the coming generation by the way we think about history" (46). While history may appear to be static and cold, it is important to remember that actual people had their lives ruined, and felt a pain that was very real. The novel reviews, "the war that was waged in 1942 and in the process of central issues of the war" (Adhikari 46). While there was much focus on the glory and heroism associated with the war, modern audiences have the potential to become distanced from the reality that once was. The story of Almasy's life and its bitter end were not uncommon for a time of war. If anything, Almasy's prolonged death is a more romanticized version of what actually happened millions of times over. Each death from the war is an actual person: a lover, a relative, a aspiring student or even a friend, swiftly ripped from the earth as if without significance. Being somewhat privileged, Almasy's removal from the world and resulting lack of engagement allow modern readers to grasp the reality of a loss of human life in slow motion. Expanding upon this understanding, Adhikari states that the novel, "not only affected the nations that were directly involved in the physical arena, but also the lives, loves, and hopes of many who were distinctly yet negatively associated with the happenings of the battlefront" (47-48). Friends and family waiting back home even had the potential for losing interest in the world, because those they loved died in battle. Oddly, pain and removal reach so far that even those who are meant to heal are hurt. For example, "Hana the nurse is herself a patient, wrecked by emotion; she too has suffered drastically with the death

181

of her father in war" (48). The idea of the hurt nurse, a paradoxical healer who is herself damaged beyond repair, demonstrates how the pain of war does not discriminate. In conclusion, Adhikari feels that *The English Patient* brings to life the, "shattered lives that the war has created" (48). Most importantly, these lives are displayed in a realistic enough manner for our modern audiences to understand. The pain of war has the ability to deeply depress and remove even the most involved people from this world. On the topic of modern audiences and their understandings of the world is the film *The Matrix*, which also deals largely with purpose and engagement.

Similar to Almasy, Neo also experiences a change in engagement in three stages. However, his changes are positive and change his life from being mundane and meaningless to purposeful. Originally, Neo was known as Mr. Anderson, a mid-level worker at a software company. Given a scene where he is lectured about job performance, it is clear that he cares little for his job. He is part of the corporate machine, or just an insignificant piece of a larger company which cares little for his existence. The height of engagement in the surface world comes when others ask him to write illegal software and hack. Even with this illegal activity, he is still without a sense of being engaged in the world and searches for a deeper meaning that he is sure exists. Evidence of this higher purpose is brought to him by Morpheus, who explains that there is thankfully more to this world than meets the eye.

Neo first endures living a purposeless life until it reaches a breaking point, and he chooses to leave it all behind. In his article "Coded Discourse: Romancing the (Electronic) Shadow in *The Matrix*," Jason Haslam explains how his choice to leave it all behind is because Neo states, "I don't like the idea that I'm not in control of my life" (96). Instead of being subject to the system, and falling into the routine of how modern life works, he would rather step out. He makes it clear that he does not want to be similar to a cog in a machine, but that he wants to control as opposed to being controlled. With that being said, Neo starts down the pash of being, "restored to life by Morpheus" (99). He is released from the surface world of being controlled and exploited. His release at the hands of Morpheus allows him to truly experience life, and not just a mere constructed reality.

Towards the beginning of the film, Neo is the epitome of being uninvolved and uncaring for the world. In "*The Matrix* and the Revolutionary Drive through "The Desert of the Real,"" by Alex Blazer, he focuses on the transition of Neo from an underground computer programmer to the savior of humanity. Examining the beginning of the film, Blazer points out that "what Neo thinks is Real is merely a symbolic construct, a virtual reality designed by what used to be our civilization's machines for the purpose of pacifying the human mind as the body is harvested as a battery to run the machines." (Blazer 266). Essentially, Neo is a not a crucial factor in the workings of his world. On the surface level, Neo, "puts on the guise of the game and leads the life of a comfortable corporate computer programmer; however, by night, he defies the system as a criminal computer hacker and dealer of illegal experience simulations" (266). However, upon viewing all three of his lives: being a corporate worker, an illegal hacker and a battery, it is clear that Neo is uninvolved and without a sense of purpose. In fact, this is what causes him to lose sleep and continuously wonder about a greater meaning. Eventually, he meets with the one person who can not only give him truth, but give him purpose: Morpheus. Their very meeting and conversation proves that Neo was not engaging the world or involved in a meaningful manner. This conversation paves the way for the next level of engagement on behalf of Neo.

In the second stage of becoming engaged with the world and finding his sense of purpose, Neo is educated on the ways of the matrix, the real world, and the connection between the two. He joins Morpheus and begins to understand how the matrix works and what it all means. Demonstrating that he is not uninterested, he listens to Morpheus and does what he tells him to. He practices in all of the training programs, willingly allows for information to be uploaded into his brain and even enters the Matrix to perform assignments. His newfound p urpose in the once pointless and meaningless world pales in comparison only to his final discovery: that he is The One. Their meeting allows for Neo to not only unlock his mind, but also to speak it.

Once the two meet, Morpheus allows for Neo to speak freely on how he feels about the world; a move that shows how little meaning Neo's life had up until that point. Referring back to Blazer's article, he explains how Morpheus starts by saying, "let me tell you why you are here. You have come because you know something. What you know you can't explain but you feel it. You've felt it your whole life" (Blazer 266). The scene shows how Neo has had a restlessness within him and a dissatisfaction with his current life. Moving forward, Blazer then focuses on the later portion of the film and how Neo's life gradually gains meaning. He states, "Neo learns from his trip down the whole that he is the most important whole; he is the One" (267). His purpose at the end of the film greatly contrasts his lack of purpose in the beginning. Eventually, he begins to, "understand how to master the Matrix" (268). Once his mastery of the matrix is complete, he realizes just how much meaning his life has. Beyond knowing what is outside of constructed reality, knowing the workings of the matrix, and mastering the matrix, he realizes that he is, "designed to bring harmony to the Matrix" (270). From start to finish, he comes to realize that instead of living a life that holds no meaning, he is actually living one that arguably has the most meaning. The result is a new level of engagement in a world for which he once had little interest.

The final stage in becoming engaged and finding purpose is the greatest in terms of what it means not simply for himself, but also the world. Discovering that he is "The One," or the one to bring harmony to the matrix, Neo realizes that he must take down the agents and save both worlds. He essentially becomes a Christ figure of great importance. The transition from start to finish, from being a skillful yet ordinary office worker to taking on the role of being the savior of the world, provides for a great deal of contrast. In an opposite manner from Almasy, he becomes increasingly engaged in the world despite its depressing condition. Through his engagement, he finds that his true purpose is not just moderately important, but that involves the fate of the world.

In the later portion of the film, Neo puts his previously learned skills to work in order to truly engage the world. Debra Shaw focuses on his new skills in "Systems, Architecture & The Digital Body: From *Alphaville* to *The Matrix.*" Fortunately for Neo, his mundane life of hacking computers and understanding code allows for him to learn how to manipulate the, "surface of everyday life" (Shaw 84). The learning of code grants him the ability to move fast, jump far and perform actions that ordinary humans are unable to. With, "the world that we take to be 'reality'" being a, "computer simulation," Neo is able to be heavily engaged thanks to his skills (81). During the heist scene, this engagement reaches a new high for Neo and his hacking capabilities. He enters the matrix, freshly, "equipped with an impressive array of virtual weaponry," and is able to, "manipulate code" (81). Where the old Mr. Anderson would never stand a chance in that situation, Neo is able to orchestrate a mission and take on enemies who once would have killed him with ease. In addition, his dedication to his new life is illustrated in a later scene where he is able to demonstrate his new skills. Shaw explains that "Neo's superadditional hacking capabilities are represented on screen by the use of special effects, including several scenes which make use of the Wachowski's 'Bullet Time' simulations" (83). His earlier identity with its lack of purpose is fully gone at this moment, and only the highly engaged Neo remains. Once Neo discovered and realized his purpose, it rendered him more engaged than he possible ever was before.

Even though *The Matrix* is a science fiction film partially set in America during the 1990s and *The English Patient* is a post-war novel set after World War II, they relate in terms of their main characters' sense of purpose and engagement in a fallen world. These two postsecular terms are major factors in the two texts, and they provide for the overall mood of the stories. In *The English Patient*, Almasy is engaged in the world and has a sense of purpose only for it to be painfully taken away from him over time. As for *The Matrix*, Neo experiences an opposite transition as he progressively becomes more involved in his world and discovers that his life has great meaning. The similarities between the texts in terms of these definitions of postsecularism illustrates how two vastly different works can actually relate.

SOURCES

Adhikari, Madhumalati. "History and Story: Unconventional History in Michael Ondaatje's *The* English Patient and James A. Michener's *Tales of the South Pacific.*" *History and Theory,* Theme Issue 41 (2002): 43-55. *MLA Bibliography.* Web. 26 Apr. 2011.

Blazer, Alex. "*The Matrix* and the Revolutionary Drive through "The Desert of the Real."" *Literature/Film Quarterly* 35.4 (2007): 265-273. *MLA Bibliography.* Web. 26 Apr. 2011.

Haslam, Jason. "Coded Discourse: Romancing the (Electronic) Shadow in *The Matrix.*" *College Literature* 32.3 (2005): 92-115. *MLA Bibliography.* Web. 26 Apr. 2011.

Jasper, David. "Wanderings in the Desert: From the Exodus to *The English Patient.*" *Literature* & *Theology* 18.2 (2004): 153-168. *MLA Bibliography.* Web. 26 Apr. 2011.

Ondaatje, Michael. *The English Patient.* New York: Vintage International, 1992. Print.

Shaw, Debra. "Systems, Architecture & The Digital Body: From *Alphaville* to *The Matrix.*" *Parallax* 14.3 (2008): 74-87. *MLA Bibliography.* Web. 26 Apr. 2011.

Shin, Andrew. "*The English Patient*'s Desert Dream." *Literature Interpretation Theory* 18 (2007): 213-236. *MLA Bibliography.* Web. 26 Apr. 2011.

The Matrix. Dir. Wachowski Brothers. Perf. Keanu Reeves, Laurence Fishburne, and Carrie-Anne Moss. Warner Bros. Pictures, 1999. Film.

21. The History and Ever-Changing Identity of Masculinity Studies
Man Without Restraint

The world of literary criticism is in a state of continual growth. Much of what exists today comes as a direct result of the studies of the past. Without these foundations being constructed over the course of years or even decades, the newly developed theories of the present may not exist as they do in their present state. For example, if it were not for emergence of feminism in the nineteenth century, the foundation for second-wave feminism in the 1960s may not have even existed. However, with not only its emergence but also its strengthening, the stage was set for another wave to sweep the country nearly a century later. As a result of feminism's ascension, the focus of some scholar's was turned towards the opposite sex, thus founding what is modern day masculinity studies. While the question remains unanswered if the emergence of masculinity studies from within feminism damaged or helped the latter, what is certain is the expansion of the field. Through the studying of masculinity, the field of gender studies is doubled in size due to its inclusion of the second sex. Since its appropriate birth from feminism, masculinity studies has taken a firm hold of academia, and appears everywhere from classrooms to anthologies. Similar to its predecessor, masculinity studies and its fluidity, ever-changing identity, definition and stereotypes are the subject of debates which span not just literature and film, but the study of societies both past and present.

The recent engagement of masculinity studies by scholars both professional and amateur is owed to gender studies, or specifically the second wave of feminism found in the mid twentieth century. However, similar to feminism, masculinity studies has also suffered from its own set of stereotypes. For example, in Rachel Adams' 2002 edition of *The Masculinity Studies Reader*, she begins the anthology with the quote, "a man never begins by presenting himself as an individual of a certain sex; it goes without saying that he is a man" (Adams 1). The quote originates from *The Second Sex* by Simone de Beauvoir, and is key in understanding the stereotypes surrounding masculinity. The quote explains a man's presence as powerful and striking, as if all who are in the company of a man are aware of that fact, and are also awe struck. Even though this idea still endures, modern masculinity studies suggests that men are no longer so easily defined. Also, Adams addresses how scholars should examine masculine identities. Early in masculinity studies, "the implicit subject of the western intellectual tradition was to concentrate on woman" (1). In other words, similar to how much of women and feminism was understood by examining their relationships with men, masculinity studies was also understood merely by its relationship with women. However, there is a "growing body of scholarship devoted to addressing this historical imbalance by locating men and masculinity as the explicit subjects of analysis" (1). This point of time in masculinity studies is one of transition, because the way it is approached by scholars and the very way it is understood is being both reinvestigated and reexamined. One key way of better understanding masculinity studies is to reexamine its history and its ascendancy into scholarly focus.

While it may first appear that masculinity and male studies have always been the focus of history, they have only been under close examination in the few decades since the rise of feminism. In the short time it has been under investigation, methods have been changed, done away with and even invented. Rachel Adams explains that "masculinity studies is a product of the major reconfiguration of academic disciplines that has taken place since the 1960s. Borders have been redrawn, new methodologies have emerged, and many of the old disciplines have been rethought and reconstituted" (1). Despite its short life, it has been subject to numerous changes both minimal and significant. Even the heightened awareness of masculinity studies has influenced its understanding. Adams states that there is, "a new self-consciousness about the theoretical and methodological

188

assumptions underlying traditional disciplinary formations" (1-2). Many narratives within masculinity studies have been dominated by handful of theories or methods, but recently these approaches have greatly changed. Additionally, even though the aforementioned quote suggests otherwise, Adams stresses that gender studies are not static. In fact, she notes that "scholars in many disciplines have sought to denaturalize de Beauvoir's observation that "it goes without saying that he is a man," by demonstrating that masculinities are constructed, mutable, and contingent, and analyzing their many and widespread effects" (2). Given their touchy nature and ability to be easily altered, it is important to grasp the concept that gender studies is a fluid entity and not one whose properties are concrete. With that being said, masculinity studies' attributes are not excluded from changes due to outside influence, and many of its properties stem from earlier feminism.

Given its rise as a result of feminism-oriented gender studies, masculinity studies shares a similar past and focus to that of feminist studies. Rachel Adams explains, "taking its lead from feminism, masculinity studies is thus dedicated to analyzing what has often seemed to be an implicit fact, that the vast majority of societies are patriarchal and that men have historically enjoyed more than their share of power, resources, and cultural authority" (2). In other words, despite their focus being on opposite sexes, feminist and masculine studies often relate due to their interest in the power of men. In addition, Adams theorizes that masculinity studies owes its existence to the relatively recent rise of feminism. She explains how, "any historical account of the field's development must commence with the ascendancy of second-wave feminism during the 1960s and the consolidation of women's studies in the academy during the next decade" (3). It is due to feminism's newfound prominence in academic settings and its near unification that masculinity studies gained its voice. The strengthening of feminist studies brought masculinity studies to light, but by the time this had occurred, it was clear that much of its history was not left intact. Adams states that studiers of masculinity wish to do as feminist theorists have and take on, "the project of historical recovery" (3). Scholars focusing on feminism wished to bring, "attention to unrecognized female authors, artists, and power political agents, as well as the previously invisible histories" (3). It can be said that modern masculinity studies not only owes its existence and current state to feminism, but also that it borrows heavily and regularly from its predecessor. The two may focus on opposite sexes, but they are one in the same, often sharing both methods and approaches.

In order to better understand the current state of modern masculinity studies, its past in relation to second-wave feminism must be examined. Rachel Adams explains how, "in the 1970s, the revolutionary import of the feminist insurgency in the streets, the voting booth, various professional arenas, and the academy was not lost on a generation of men who had been either actively involved with or sympathetic to the New Left" (4). Meaning that, when this wave of feminism rose up significantly and was found prospering in various locations throughout our society, a sizable number of men were right alongside them helping these women ascend. The rise of feminism in the twentieth century was not a solitary project in which only women contributed to its success. In fact, men played a moderate role in the process. After the rise of feminism was secured for the most part, many men in addition to male and female scholars began to turn their gaze towards masculinity studies. Additionally, the resulting rise of masculinity studies was not only helped by the existence of the feminist movement, but was aided by the gay rights movement as well. Adams explains the situation in stating, "although this early men's movement was primarily a response to feminism, its political urgency was undoubtedly heightened by the emergency of the gay liberation movement at the end of the 1960s" (5). With these two somewhat unexpected allies helping secure its ascension, masculinity studies was well on the way to being brought into mainstream public consciousness. In addition to being related to both the feminist and gay rights movements in terms of its ascension, the rise of masculinity studies shares similar traits in its mechanics.

With masculine studies being brought into mainstream public consciousness, it began to be tackled by scholars, show up in academics and take on a new shape. Adams explains, "at the same time that the first-wave men's movement was consolidating, scholars in a number of disciplines began to introduce the critique of patriarchal masculinities into their work" (5). Similar to feminist studies, masculinity studies began to firmly plant itself in academia with the attention of scholars from various fields of study. Although, the work surrounding masculinity studies in this time period is typically not without praise for its predecessor. Adams explains that work on masculine studies, "repeatedly acknowledges its debt to feminism" (5). Yet, despite the many thanks for establishing the foundation on which masculinity studies would rise, these works were also thankful for many men. Work was sometimes dedicated, "to the male audience that had largely been neglected by feminist discussions of gender" (6). In other words, while it was undoubtedly grateful for all feminist studies had done, masculinity studies sought to target and thank those left unremembered after their predecessor's rise. Given its ever-changing identity and focus, masculine studies has been in a constant state of transformation ever since its late twentieth century rise.

Unlike its identity during the earlier portion of its rise, present day masculinity studies is subject to debate which leaves questions unanswered. Later in time, some scholars fully rejected previous approaches to masculinity studies by suggesting their own. Adams states that "unlike the masculinity studies that emerged during the late 1980s, most of these critics implicitly or pointedly rejected psychoanalytical accounts of gender, preferring to understand sexual oppression in the context of economic and social history" (5). While these newer approaches are perfectly acceptable, it leaves some scholars questioning the validity of such approaches as well as their usefulness in comparison to older approaches. No matter the answer, what matters is that present day masculinity studies, thanks to there being so many approaches, is more widespread than ever. Adams makes note that "evidence for the rapid spread of masculinity studies during the last decade of the twentieth century is everywhere in the many academic conferences, topical anthologies, and courses now being offered on masculinity" (7). This realization illustrates both the success of masculinity studies, and its exponential growth. However, despite its success and new approaches, one question still remains, "does masculinity studies represent a beneficial extension of feminist analysis or does it represent a hijacking of feminism?" (7). With its rise stemming from feminist studies, did masculine studies end up helping its predecessor or hurting it severely? This question is open-ended with much evidence to support either side of the argument. On one hand, the rise of masculinity studies helped to double the size of gender studies with its inclusion of the other sex. However, on the other hand, it is argued that the desperately needed attention on feminist studies was prematurely stolen away, if even partially. Rachel Adams' question is where many who judge the history of masculinity studies are left stuck in debate, but what is unarguable is its presence within present day.

In Stephen M. Whitehead's 2001 edition of *The Masculinities Reader*, an anthology comprised of numerous essays on masculinity studies, one of the key issues tackled is "masculinism." In his essay titled "Masculinities and Masculinism," Arthur Brittan explains the behavioral issues of men, the ever-changing nature of masculinity and its relationship with all outside forces by which it is influenced. Brittan states that "how men behave will depend upon the existing social relations of gender. By this I mean the way in which men and women confront each other ideologically and politically" (Brittan 52). Similar to the idea that it is impossible to be a rebel, because a rebel's defiant actions are solely defined by their opposition to the dominant narrative, the behavior of men is defined by women. The dominant narrative which defines how a man should act is altered and modified in direct relation to how women act. To further explain his belief, Brittan explains, "gender is never simply an arrangement in which the roles of men and women are decided in a contingent and haphazard way. At any given moment, gender will reflect the material interests of those who have power and those who do not" (52). In other words, current behavioral traits found in men were not always this way. Whoever happens to control the dominant narrative in society also greatly influences the direction and identity of masculinity. Outside of the influence of the dominant narrative, masculinity studies is also influenced by other forces. Brittan states that masculinity, "does not exist in isolation from femininity – it will always be an expression of the current image that men have of themselves in relation to women. And these images are often contradictory and ambivalent" (52). This theory illustrates how man's idea of masculinity changes so much in relation to femininity that it even has the potential to contradict itself and disprove or put into jeopardy what it once established. On the subject of change, Brittan delves further into masculinity's inability to never set still.

Continuing where Rachel Adams' thoughts on change within masculinity left off, Brittan examines the mechanics of change itself. He explains that while masculinity never changes in that it, "is always local and subject to change," it is this process of change that is so thought provoking. Brittan explains how there are different methods of change, and that some changes are differently timed than others. He explains this by stating, "some masculinities are long-lived, whilst others are as ephemeral as fads in pop music. However, what does not easily change is the justification and naturalization of male power; that is, what remains relatively constant in masculine ideology, masculinism or heterosexualism." (52-53). He explains how masculinity is able to experience changes both swift and lengthy, yet also contains elements which are seemingly invulnerable to change. After giving examples of aspects which never seem to change and others which change swiftly, Brittan explains how certain portions of masculinity change over a great length of time. He explains that "masculinity refers to those aspects of men's behavior that fluctuate over time. In some cases these fluctuations may last for decades – in others it may be a matter of weeks or months" (53). An example of a change which takes decades to occur is male style. Both the hairstyles of men and general fashion have changed greatly over the past few decades, consisting of styles that look feminine, stereotypically masculine and even androgynous. Brittan notes how, after this great amount of change, "male identity is a fragile and tentative thing with no secure anchorage in the contemporary world" (53). Present day masculinity is unique in the sense that goes beyond traditional uniqueness. It is no longer a well defined and easily explained pattern of changes unique to the changes found before it, but is instead at a point where it can be anything for absolutely no reason. Twenty first century masculinity is seemingly in a world of its own, where identity is difficult to accurately pinpoint.

Elwood Watson's anthology *Performing American Masculinities: The 21st-Century Man in Popular Culture* attempts to explore present day masculine studies in order to better define what some scholars refer to as a spontaneous masculinity outside of explanation and prediction. Margaret C. Ervin's essay "The Might of the Metrosexual" focuses on the modern man, and contrasts it with traditional masculinity. She explains how there are two narratives within masculinity: the dominant narrative which has been around for some time, and the modern narrative. Ervin explains how some authors have written comical works on the difference between the two. She states how she examined the supposed threat to masculinity in, "a guidebook parody titled *The Badass Bible*. It portrays the threats posed to traditional masculinity, or "badass" masculinity" (Ervin 67). Acting like a "badass" is the type of behavior that most associate with traditional masculinity. However, given modern day masculinity's ability to be unpredictable, "many of the rules set down in this handbook deal with the necessity to act spontaneously" (67). However, it is stressed that "by virtue of the fact that the book is a parody, the notion is mocked." (67). In other words, *The Badass Bible* is aware of trends in modern masculinity, and therefore uses this heightened awareness for the purpose of comedy. After poking fun at these new trends in masculinity, the text then jokingly attempts to reestablish a more traditional dominant narrative by providing, "a depiction of the badass, the avatar of hegemonic masculinity" (67). While it may seem that the focus of the text is purely to be comical, it is not. Ervin explains that there are many opportunities to study the text for a deeper truth, as opposed to merely admiring the jokes which it provides. She states that there is the "potential of the unattainability of badass stature" (67). This statement is true because such status is absolutely absurd. According to Ervin, the very notion of becoming the type of badass the traditional narrative has established is nearly impossible due to the requirements. She explains how "*The Badass Bible* makes it clear that being a badass is all about being ready for a fight, not necessarily starting the fight, but being ready to physically retaliate for the slightest cause" (67). This idea is not only legitimately dangerous and jeopardizing of self-preservation, it is self-destructive. In conclusion, while the traits of the modern day man and the metrosexual strongly go against what it traditionally means to be a man, any comparison of the two helps further validate the former. The spontaneity and seemingly unpredictable behavior of the modern man is safer, less absurd and much more easily obtainable than that of stereotypical man.

Venturing deeply into the field of film and cinema, Peter Lehman's anthology *Masculinity: Bodies, Movies, Culture* relates current theories in masculinity to modern movies. Krin Gabbard's "Someone is Going to Pay: Resurgent White Masculinity in *Ransom*" investigates instances of masculinity in contemporary cinema. She notes how, despite modern man's unpredictability and spontaneity, some behavior is still easily understood. For example, she explains how, "an early scene in *Ransom* (directed by Ron Howard in 1996) presents an image that powerfully symbolizes the masculine anxieties of both the hero and the film" (Gabbard 7). Interestingly, the creators of the film do not disguise these anxieties or attempt to make them more subtle. Instead, Gabbard feels as if they are blatantly presented. She recalls a scene, explaining, "with its two large circular balloons, the contraption is also a metaphor for Tom's prominent but threatened masculinity: his "balls"" (8). The scene which Gabbard explains is one featuring the kidnapping of a man's child. Once the man's son is kidnapped and taken by the film's antagonists, the obviously arranged balloons pop due to being struck. In addition, she explains that there are further allusions to men being without their testicles, or their manhood. Gabbard makes the point, "because of the long association of hair with sexuality, baldness often symbolizes castration" (16). While this instance of male anxiety is more subtle than the last, the two are still quite blatantly presented for anyone with a mild knowledge of film to recognize. Gabbard's review of the film *Ransom* illustrates that, while it is in a difficult to define state of fluctuating identity, masculinity is still sometimes traditionally presented in select forms of media. At this moment, it is in a state where it shares pieces of the old and new blended together to create a unique whole.

Modern masculinity studies not only owes its existence to second-wave feminism, it also shares many traits with its predecessor. With its nearly impossible to concretely define identity, fluid nature and application to numerous academic studies, masculinity studies is often the subject of investigation and close examination. Even the change found within masculinity is studied intensely, because of its ability to be both lengthy and quite fast. In fact, it is not guaranteed that change even occurs at all for certain aspects of masculinity. While styles and behavior often change, certain insecurities and anxieties seem to persist. Moreover, similar to the very nature of change within itself, present day masculinity is at a unique state, because of its nearly seamless inclusion of elements from both the past and present. Since the heightening of the mainstream public's awareness of the issue, masculinity studies has permeated its way into many fields of study in a way strikingly similar to that of women's studies.

SOURCES

Adams, Rachel and David Savran, eds. *The Masculinity Studies Reader*. Malden, Massachusetts: Blackwell Publishers, 2002. Print.

Brittan, Arthur. "Masculinities and Masculinism." *The Masculinities Reader*. Ed. Stephen M. Whitehead. Malden, Massachusetts: Polity Press, 2001. 51-55. Print.

Ervin, Margaret C. "The Might of the Metrosexual." Performing American Masculinities: The 21st-Century Man in Popular Culture. Ed. Elwood Watson. Bloomington, Indiana: Indiana University Press, 2011. 58-75. Print.

Gabbard, Krin. "Someone is Going to Pay: Resurgent White Masculinity in *Ransom*." *Masculinity: Bodies, Movies, Culture*. Ed. Peter Lehman. New York: Routledge, 2001. 7-24. Print.

SOURCE CONSULTED

Silverman, Kaja. "Masochism and Male Subjectivity." *The Masculinity Studies Reader*. Eds. Rachel Adams and David Savran. Malden, Massachusetts: Blackwell Publishers, 2002. 21-40. Print.

EPILOGUE

"The Men of the Valley and Their Defining Masochism"

It's typically an unoriginal move to begin a piece of prose with the weather, but that is where the days of my valley's men begin. Every morning, no matter what the weather, and no matter the gleeful faces of young children who had recently discovered that school was canceled, these men ventured out into the fields. Across the fields they rode, often by tractor or by all-terrain vehicle. When the snow drifted in heights of feet, they sucked their lips through their teeth and rode onward, and upward. This valley was a land well within definition. Despite the grays of the passing snow, the valley was an area of concrete definition. It was an idea where, no matter what their critics might say, men were men, and women did their own thing. Within this realm of the man was early mornings, crisp gloves and hardened denim coats. The sun itself remained restful and drowsy while the men of the valley took watch over the world and of nature. However, despite all of this, in the same area of the same valley, rested me. It was wintertime, and like the animals would do, I hibernated in the comfort of my house until my body was so numb from the slumber that the states of sleep and awake seemed to be one in the same. They were indistinguishable. It is in these moments that I came to learn just what I had become: something less than a man, but not quite feminine enough to take on the role of a female. In my complacency I had become an ambiguous and androgynous figure. Less than a man, but not outside the realm of manhood. In this land of definition, where men were men, I had not suffered long enough to fit the role of man, and they knew it.

Having grown up in the rural town of Newark Valley, much of the local economy was based not off of heightening technology, but basic mechanics. Farm equipment could be spotted on just about every field, and, when not hard at work, the men of the valley sought to prolong their suffering a few steps further. At some point after the 1960's, when there had been an explosion of technology in the world, a massive fissure was created in the workforce of rural towns such as mine. While some men set out to work technical jobs, the men who were left outdated sought to retain a sort of pride in failing to keep up with the modernization of the country. In a state of protest, these men reattached themselves to classical ways of living. One of the most basic, of course, is agriculture. Even though the work is rewarding, it requires long hours in risky settings. So risky, in fact, that errors on the job could result in losing a limb or one's life. But see, instead of fleeing from such an environment for better working conditions, the men of the valley turned these horrors into a source of pride. Backbreaking conditions and horrific injuries became talking points, or even bragging points, and badges of honor. The worse the injury, the better the reputation. If one was lucky enough, they would achieve what an ancient Spartan used to call a "glorious death," or death in battle. Once in every few years, word would spread throughout the valley that a man had achieved a glorious death, or had been killed in doing farm work. He would be enshrined in the minds of male youths as the ultimate man. He who had suffered the most.

An interesting part of suffering within the valley is its redeeming quality. Similar to the tales of glad poverty passed around medieval Europe, where dirt poor beggars would cherish their poorness, the working class men of the valley would boast about their suffering. For every hour of overtime worked was another bragging point. This intentional suffering was no longer a sign of stupidity or futility, but rather an indicator of masculinity. It is within the decades after the technology revolution that these men would come to create their own definitions. There were men, and there were real men. Males who existed somewhere roughly outside of the grip of feminization were men. They suffered minimally, or rather, not as much as they could have. On the other hand are real men. Real men, so they are defined in the valley, get up out of bed, throw their work boots on, and set out to tire themselves into an exhaustion-based stupor. With each passing shift, they strengthen their image as the sufferer of the household. May no man match their own suffering.

The entire process of suffering is an extensive one, finely tuned over decades thanks to the tailoring of their own images in order to achieve the best response. The entirety of the process exists in a state of protest; that working harder instead of smarter is far more redeeming, almost to the point of being cleansing. The process has many stages, and each deserves the full attention of the man: education, wealth and mindset.

First off, a real man must flex his physical muscles, not his brain. If he is to sell his audience the idea of his suffering, he must blatantly display that he is indeed physically exhausted. Venturing into higher education and experiencing this same level of brutal exhaustion on a mental level is self-defeating, because it is a state of tired that is not so easily noticed by a judgmental audience. The real man must commit to long hours of farm work, or stay at the local factory for some overtime pay. Having time for leisure and enjoyment is a trait reserved for women and children, and lesser males. Coinciding with this is the idea that less wealth is as redeeming as hard labor. Rather than having enough money to live comfortably and be prepared for hardships, there is an emphasis on having just enough. The idea of just scraping by is romanticized in rural areas, especially through the use of country music stations on the radio. Country music, or the blues for white folks, is the music of choice for real men. Rather than enjoying music that has an uplifting message, real men choose to buy into music that showcases alcoholism, depression, adversity and stereotypical rural culture. The result of this grand routine is that real men have achieved a renaming of themselves. Their self-definition has been pinpointed and customized over the years to the point where it has become a retreat for rural-based insecure white folk. To combat the insecurity that lingers from being left behind after the progression of culture, a real man must intentionally suffer to the point where he is a lesser educated, ill-fashioned, broken and depressed person whose dreams have been cut off by the looming presence of long work hours and financial debt. This is the supposed definition of a man: the sufferer.

ABOUT THE AUTHOR

Charles Hollenbeck is a doctoral candidate at the Union Institute Graduate School, first and foremost, and an occasional author, proofreader, and editor. He received his first proofreading and editing job while working for the Cortland Writers Association; a grouping of literature students tasked with overseeing the completion of *Transition* literary magazine. Qualifying him to take up a position on the editorial board were his first two publications, *Eight & One* and *Sixteen & One*, respectively. With his first two texts being heavily based on an assortment of rhyme schemes, the position's duties came naturally. Working on *Transition* for over two years would lead to future editorial board positions for *SOAR: Student Observation & Research* Academic Journal, *Bedlam & Repose* Literary Magazine, and *Penumbra: An Interdisciplinary Journal of Critical and Creative Inquiry*. Additionally, Charles has published six pieces of poetry as well as five texts, most of which revolve around and are highly critical of gender and social relations. *From Within the Borderland* continues the pattern by investigating and examining the neurosexism and invisible structures situated in and around masculinity studies. Having been raised in the hyper-masculine area that is Upstate New York, Charles witnessed firsthand the intersection in between the immaterial and physical in regards to gender and social structures. From birth, the children of these polarized areas have their brains hardwired on how to act, perform, and even dream; a process which renders notions, thoughts, expectations and other immaterial things into physical borders and boundaries. *From Within the Borderland* reports on the many appearances and personalities of masculinity studies, from its relationship with feminism to its varying interpretations and representations. What results of this glance at modern masculinity is a reinforced stance that gender and its narratives are immaterial entities whose physical roots and supplements are plucked from thin air and the imaginations of dominant and controlling bodies. The narratives guiding modern masculinity are in a state of automation, being both minimally affected by exterior forces and outside of legitimate impact.